BALL'S BLUFF

For McKENZIE FARWELL

BALL'S BLUFF

A Small Battle and Its Long Shadow

EPM

PUBLICATIONS, INC., McLEAN, VIRGINIA

Library of Congress Cataloging-in-Publication Data

Farwell, Byron.
  Balls Bluff: a small battle and its long shadow / Byron Farwell.
    p.   cm.
  Includes bibliographical references.
  ISBN 0-939009-36-6
  1. Ball's Bluff, Battle of, 1862.   I. Title.
E472.63.F37   1990
973.7'31--dc20   90-30049
                                                                  CIP

All Rights Reserved
EPM Publications, Inc., 1003 Turkey Run Road
  McLean, VA 22101
Printed in the United States of America

Cover and book design by Tom Huestis

Contents

Books by Byron Farwell

The Man Who Presumed: A Biography of Henry M. Stanley. Henry Holt, New York, 1957. Longmans Green, London, 1958. Reprinted by Greenwood Press, Westport, CT, 1974. Paperback: Norton, New York, 1989. Translated into Swedish (1960) and Japanese (1960). Also made into a Talking Book for the blind.

Burton: A Biography of Sir Richard Francis Burton. Henry Holt, New York, 1964. Longmans Green, London, 1963. Paperbacks: Avon, New York, 1965 and Penguin, London, in 1990. Reprinted by Greenwood Press, Westport, CT, 1975. New edition by Viking in London and New York, 1988. Also published in braille.

Prisoners of the Madhi. Harper & Row, New York, 1967. Longmans Green, London, 1967. Paperbacks: Tower, New York, 1971 and Norton, New York, 1989.

Queen Victoria's Little Wars. Harper & Row, New York, 1972. Allen Lane/ The Penguin Press, London, 1973. Paperback: W.W. Norton, New York, 1985.

The Great Anglo-Boer War. Harper & Row, New York, 1976. Published in the United Kingdom under the title *The Great Boer War* by Allen Lane/ The Penguin Press, London, 1977. Paperback: Norton, New York, 1990.

Mr. Kipling's Army. W.W. Norton, New York, 1981. Published in the United Kingdom under the title *For Queen and Country* by Allen Lane/ The Penguin Press, London, 1981. Paperback: W.W. Norton, New York, 1987.

The Gurkhas. W.W. Norton, New York, 1984. Allen Lane/ The Penguin Press, London, 1984. Paperback: Penguin, 1985, and Norton, 1990.

Eminent Victorian Soldiers: Seekers of Glory. W.W. Norton, New York, 1985. Viking, London, 1986. Paperback: W.W. Norton, 1988.

The Great War in Africa, 1914–1918. W.W. Norton, New York, 1986. Viking, London, 1987. Paperback: W.W. Norton, 1989.

Armies of the Raj: From the Great Indian Mutiny to Independence, 1858–1947. W.W. Norton, New York, 1989. Viking, London, 1990.

Ball's Bluff: A Small Battle and Its Long Shadow. Paperback original: EPM Publications, McLean, VA., 1990.

FOREWORD

Histories of wars move from battle to battle; accounts of battles end when the last shot is fired, the last sword sheathed. But battles are not really ended when the smoke clears and the clamor ceases. The dead must be disposed of, the wounded carried off and cared for, anxious relatives and friends must be comforted or reassured, prisoners of war must be marched off to prisons, rewards or rebukes given, and the military and political consequences assessed.

The Battle of Ball's Bluff, fought near Leesburg, Virginia on October 21, 1861, was a battle neither side intended or wanted to fight; yet, like a perfect Greek tragedy, it had a distinct beginning, middle and end. It was, as battles go, a small affair, yet it contained all of the elements of larger battles in any era, a full measure of pity and terror, courage and cowardice, exultation and pain, carnage and close encounters, cruelties, coincidences and bizarre happenings.

Although of no strategic importance, its participants re-membered it as one of the most vital and most memorable events in their lives, and at the time it was widely regarded, in both North and South, as a momentous occurrence. The political consequences of this small battle were enormous for the North, and for many of the Union survivors. Yet the complete story of the battle and its aftermath has never been told, and much of what has been written about it is erroneous.

A great battle is really a series of small battles that take place at about the same time in about the same place. One man's experience can be the opposite of another's, and no one man, not even the commanders, can encompass all of its happenings or its experiences. The Battle of Ball's Bluff, how-ever, can be seen as a simply constructed human drama–a tragedy, as all battles are—on a scale all can comprehend. What each person did had significance, and each person's experiences formed important elements of the battle.

The Ball's Bluff battlefield can still be seen; a historical marker on Route 15 north of Leesburg directs the curious to the bluff. The area where the most severe fighting took place is now heavily wooded, but at the spot where the narrow road leading to the battlefield ends there is a small clearing. There, surrounded by a low wall, in the smallest of all our national cemeteries, twenty-five headstones stand. Only one records a name. In the grass outside the wall stands a memorial to a Confederate color bearer who fell in the battle and a stone erected by unknown hands purporting to mark the spot where Colonel Baker was killed.

A path through the woods leads to a spot where one can see the steepness of the bluff and almost the whole of Harrison's Island, from which the Federals embarked for Virginia. Across the river one can walk the towpath of the C&O Canal and see the remains of locks and buildings at Edwards Ferry, which figured so prominently in Union strategy.

Although the counties on both sides of the river have increased their populations enormously in the past 130 years, the banks of the Potomac here are depopulated. Gone is the canal traffic and the many roads that ran to the canal and parallel to it; gone, too, are the many mills which in 1861 graced its shores. Only one commercial ferry still plies back and forth across the river and the numerous, once busy fords are used no longer.

If one visits the area on a fine day in late October, the view from above or below the bluff, or across the river, is much the same as it was in 1861. The river still flows, the maple trees still flame, the farmland on Harrison's Island is still cultivated. Fort Evans, the earthwork that was Confederate headquarters, still stands well preserved, as do some Confederate trenches, although these are on private property. In

Leesburg, Virginia, and Poolesville, Maryland, there are buildings that were standing in 1861, and throughout Loudoun County, still lived in, are many 19th- and even 18th-century houses and numerous log cabins. In spite of encroaching real estate development, it is easy to feel how it once was.

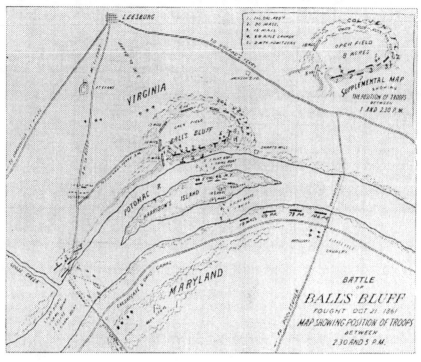

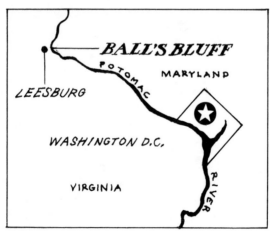

1.
A Prelude to War
✳ ✳ ✳

It had been a beautiful October day. Mr. Lincoln commented on it to newspaper reporters as about sunset he walked into General McClellan's headquarters in Washington, a fine residence on Jackson Square. To one reporter, Charles Carlton Coffin, it seemed that the lines in the president's face were deeper, his cheeks more sunken than usual. A battle was taking place only thirty-five miles up river on the Virginia shore at a place called Ball's Bluff. Colonel Edward ("Ned") Baker, an intimate friend of the president, was in command of the Federal troops engaged.

As Lincoln entered McClellan's headquarters the telegraph keys were clicking, and the news they carried was not good. The battle was still in progress, but less than two hours earlier Ned Baker had been killed. When the president was handed the message announcing his death, he stood stunned, not speaking or moving for several minutes. Then he crossed the room towards the door, walking alone, his head bowed. As he stepped into the street, he stumbled and nearly fell. Bystanders noticed that his chest was heaving, and there were tears rolling down his rutted face as, holding both hands to his breast, he walked slowly down the street.

The date was October 21, 1861. The war had barely begun to take its toll of friends and enemies alike, but Ned Baker had been something special, and the president's second son, Edward Baker Lincoln (1846-1850) had been named after him.

Edward Dickinson Baker was born in England in 1811, the son of a schoolmaster, and was brought to the United States by his Quaker parents when he was four years old. At fourteen he was apprenticed to a weaver, but he was, it seems, already possessed of higher ambitions, for Lincoln liked to tell the story of how, when Baker was a boy, he was found crying his heart out because he had just discovered that, not being a native American, he could not be president.

He did not long remain a weaver's apprentice. At nineteen he qualified to practice law and at twenty he married a widow two years older than he who already had two children. He settled in Carrollton, Illinois and joined the Disciples of Christ–then called "Campbellites." It was in the church that he discovered his remarkable oratorical talents, and it was his ability as an extemporaneous speaker that was to constitute his passport to success.

All who knew Baker remarked upon the quality of his voice. Charles Sumner described it as "not full or sonorous, but . . . sharp and clear. It was penetrating rather than commanding, and yet when touched by his ardent nature, it became sympathetic and even musical." Senator O.H. Browning also spoke of "the melody of his voice" and "the witchery of the spell" he was able to cast over his hearers. Carrollton was too small for his talents and in 1835 he moved to Springfield, where he practiced law and made friends with Abraham Lincoln. At age twenty-six he entered the Illinois legislature; three years later he was a state senator.

Baker had that combination of natural and acquired talents that made him a successful politician in nineteenth-century America: pleasant manners, personal charm and a memory for names and faces. He loved to be with people, to feel their response to his personality, to sway masses with his eloquence, to touch the hearts of men in crowds and carry them with him down a stream of dreams, sentiment and elevated passion to political conviction. Although Baker was born British, the

United States held no more ardent patriot. He wore his patriotism like a bright cloak. He believed in progress, expanding commerce and the "manifest destiny" of America. If his idealism and his beliefs seemed simple and shallow, always on the surface, they were no less real to him, for he lived on the surface of life and delighted in it. And if he carried always a fine opinion of himself, he was no different from any politician in any age, for fine opinions of one's worth, unshakably held, are essential for such men's survival.

Baker loved to recite poetry, and he was a restless and incurable romantic. Martial glory loomed large in his dreams. He had been elected a lieutenant by his company in the Black Hawk War, and in Springfield he formed a militia company and became its captain. In 1844 the governor appointed him a colonel of militia, and two years later he raised a regiment, the 4th Illinois Volunteers, for the war in Mexico. Years later he described his motivation: "I went there, as I think, impelled by motives of patriotism, having mingled with it not a little desire for adventure, love of change and that feverish excitement for which we people of this country are always and everywhere remarkable."

Baker was twice wounded in the Mexican War: he was stabbed by a bayonet while quelling a riot among Georgia volunteers, and at the battle of Cerro Gordo his lungs were pierced by a piece of grape shot while leading an impetuous charge. He was ever after called "Colonel" Baker, and he often spoke of how he had served "in a foreign land beneath the Stars and Stripes of my country." In 1848 he was elected to Congress and soon Lincoln and other congressmen were urging president Zachary Taylor to give him a cabinet post. Taylor refused.

In 1852 Baker took his family to San Francisco, where he established a thriving law practice, and in 1854 he entered into partnership with Isaac Wistar. Although Wistar was sixteen years younger than Baker, he proved a valuable partner

14

in peace and in war, for he was, as Baker was not, meticulous and methodical. Baker never kept accurate accounts and did not even keep a docket of his cases. He never formally prepared for court, and he carried such papers as were necessary in his hat, relying on his exceptional memory for the data he needed. He was paid fine fees, but he loved to gamble at faro and he was a spendthrift, frequently unable to pay his bills. Still, he was known to give a $20 gold piece to a beggar in a grand, impetuous gesture.

Baker had always been a Whig, but, like Lincoln, he switched his allegiance to the Republican party after it was founded in 1854. In 1859 a delegation of Republicans in Oregon invited him to move to that state and to be their candidate for the United States Senate. The following year he moved his family there, and in October he was elected a senator. In Washington he became one of Lincoln's stoutest supporters. At the beginning of the war, when president Lincoln was criticized for some of his dictatorial actions, Baker rose up on the Senate floor to say that he approved of all that Lincoln did: "I want sudden, bold, forward, determined war; and I do not think anybody can conduct war of that kind as well as a dictator." In turn, the president also thought highly of Baker and sought his advice more often than he did that of most members of his cabinet. When war came, Baker was not content, as were so many of his colleagues in the Congress, to wage war merely with words: although his brown hair had turned to silver and he was fifty years old, he volunteered his services. Limited as his experience of war had been, it was

---

Abraham Lincoln named his second son after old friend and ally Edward D. Baker, the charming, eloquent senator from Oregon. Although his military experience was limited, Baker received a commission as colonel when the Civil War began and was the senior U.S. officer on the field at Ball's Bluff.

still more than most of the politicians who donned uniforms could claim, and he offered to raise his own regiment.

Baker's regiment was a peculiar one. It is difficult for most Americans today to realize how great were the regional differences of a century ago. Americans were not then so mobile; most lived and died in the county or at least the state in which they were born. The *esprit de clocher* was strong. People wanted to be with their own kind, and their own kind were people from their town or county. When a Minnesota regiment camped beside a Massachusetts regiment, the men in each were curious about the other, for they had different speech patterns and different habits; they came from different clans of the same tribe. American culture was not then the homogenous conglomerate it has since become. States' rights meant more than legal or legislative rights, and more than attitudes towards Blacks. There was thought to be a state culture–a particular kind of life, a way of looking at ideas and events, a pattern of life that was, or was considered to be, unique to each state.

Volunteer regiments sought social cohesion, and most found it in simple geography. A regiment came from one city or one county, and within the regiment were formed companies from one town or one section of a city. The men knew each other; they knew their officers. Long after the war, General Francis Walker, who had begun the war as a private in the 15th Massachusetts, remembered how it was: "Why, in those days, hardly one of our number would have thought that he could bring his mind to enlist in a strange regiment, or even in another company from that to which his schoolmates and his townsmen belonged."

Other regiments were formed around a cultural affinity. Tammany Hall raised a regiment; there were regiments of German immigrants and of men from Ireland or of Irish descent. But one of the most curious of bases was provided by a group in New York City who set out to raise a regiment

16

composed of men who had once lived in California. By the end of April 1861, the organizers had signed up a couple of hundred men, and they had asked Senator Edward Baker to be their colonel.

Although the idea originated in New York, only one company originated there (Company G); another was formed in Washington, D.C. (Company R). The remaining companies came from Philadelphia. Baker was too busy in the Senate to spend time actively recruiting, so his former law partner in California, Isaac Wistar, now in Philadelphia, did the work for him and became the regiment's lieutenant colonel. Recalling his recruiting efforts years later, Wistar said he couldn't remember "how many drinks of bad whiskey I was obliged to consume and bestow in the service of my country; but on the second night I took one hundred men to New York by the midnight emigrant train, at the fare of a dollar a head, which was my pecuniary tribute to the cause."

The 1st California, as the regiment called itself, was the first of the three-year enlistment regiments to complete its organization, and it was at the time the only federally sponsored regiment of volunteer infantry. When Governor A.G. Curtin of Pennsylvania protested against the recruiting of Pennsylvanians by "outsiders" and when real California units began to be formed on the West Coast, the regiment became officially the 71st Pennsylvania and finally a part of the Philadelphia Brigade, although it continued to be called, even in official reports, the 1st California or simply the California Regiment. Among the officers were Baker's brother, Dr. Alfred Baker; his son, Second Lieutenant Edward Baker, Jr.; and a nephew, Second Lieutenant Edward B. Jerome, a son of his sister Rebecca.

The regiment formed at Fort Schuyler in the Bronx, where it was issued muskets and confiscated grey uniforms, which a southern artillery unit had ordered made in New York. Baker took little part in the organizing, equipping and drilling of his regiment. The routine of camp life bored him, and he did not care for the rigors and joys it provided. He came to New York for a few days, but slept and took his meals at the Hotel Astor.

Baker was appointed a brigadier general, but he refused the appointment. Members of congress could hold military ranks and remain senators or representatives only if they held rank below that of general officer. Baker preferred to be both a senator and a colonel. Until Congress recessed, he spent most of his time in 1861 in the Senate.

On August 1, 1861, Baker provided the Senate with one of its most dramatic incidents of that session when he strode onto the floor in his new uniform, placed his sword across his desk, and proceeded to denounce and damn Senator John C. Breckinridge of Kentucky. Breckinridge, a former vice president, had said that he preferred to see "a peaceful separation of the states" rather than "endless, devastating war." Baker was enraged. His melodious voice filled the Senate chamber as he launched a savage attack: "Are not the speeches of the senator from Kentucky intended for disorganization? Are they not intended to destroy our zeal? Are they not intended to animate our enemies? Sir, are they not words of brilliant, polished treason even in the very capitol of the republic?" Senator Charles Sumner said of that now forgotten speech that it "passed at once into the permanent literature of the country." Shortly after, Breckinridge decamped from Washington and went south to join the Confederate army.

Earlier, before the cannon blast at Fort Sumter announced the opening of the war, on that March day in Washington when Abraham Lincoln took the oath of office as president of a precariously united group of American states, Senator Baker, with Senator Franklin Pierce, rode in a barouche facing Lincoln and James Buchanan down Pennsylvania Avenue to the Capitol. On this occasion, for the first time in the nation's history, the president's escort was a mounted and armed guard instead of an honorary escort, and the carriage was surrounded by jingling, dancing cavalry. Colonel Charles P. Stone, in charge of the escort and riding alongside, used his spurs to make his horse and the horses of his men move so erratically that the president would be a difficult target for a hidden marksman. Neither Senator Ned Baker nor Colonel Charles Stone then realized how inextricably their fates would soon be entwined.

Charles Pomeroy Stone was born in Greenfield, Massachusetts, into a family whose members had fought for the United States in all its wars. He went to the United States Military Academy at West Point and was graduated in 1845, standing seventh in a class of forty-one. Two years after graduation, he saw action for the first time in the Mexican War, serving with distinction and winning two brevets. After the war and the return of the army from Mexico, Stone took two years' leave of absence to travel in Europe and the Middle East, polishing his French and studying "the numerous active armies of Europe, Syria and Egypt."

In November 1856, Stone resigned his commission and opened a bank in San Francisco. It is probable that he and Baker first met in California, for Isaac Wistar, Baker's law partner, knew Stone well at this time. Stone's bank failed when his treasurer absconded with the money. He then took up prospecting for minerals in Mexico, but again without great success.

On New Year's Eve, 1860, he was in Washington, D.C., and he stopped in at Wormley's Hotel to pay a call on his old commander, seventy-five-year-old Winfield Scott, General-in-Chief of the United States Army. Scott was a fine old soldier, but always vain and now grossly fat, a great hulk of a man, old-fashioned, no longer sharp-witted, yet wise and knowledgeable and, for the moment, still a power in Washington. The regular army Scott commanded was small— 16,367 officers and men—scattered about the country; most were in the Far West.

Stone and Scott chatted about the past, of the Mexican

19

More than most, Charles P. Stone had the potential for greatness during the Civil War. His family had a proud military history; he had been graduated near the top of his class at West Point; and he had served with distinction in the Mexican War. The Ball's Bluff affair ended his promising career.

War, and about the present, of the policy of reconciliation then being pursued by the administration. president James Buchanan firmly believed that the southern states had no legal right to secede; on the other hand, he did not believe that the federal government had a right to stop them if they did. But Buchanan was a lame duck president, and in a few months Lincoln would replace him. The two men talked of what might happen to Washington, situated as it was on the very border of Northern and Southern sentiment, should the differences between the North and the South not be reconciled. The conversation seemed ended when Scott looked at his watch, heaved his huge bulk from his chair and said that he had an appointment with the president. Stone accompanied him to the door, and while waiting for his carriage to be brought around, Scott asked, "How is the feeling in the District of Columbia? What proportion of the population would sustain the government, by force if necessary?"

"It is my belief, General," Stone replied, "that two-thirds of the fighting stock of this population would sustain the government in defending itself if called upon. But they are uncertain as to what can be done or what the government wants done, and they have no rallying point."

The carriage arrived and Stone accompanied the old general as he moved ponderously toward it. Just before entering his carriage, Scott turned to Stone and put his hand on his shoulder. "These people have no rallying point. Make yourself that rallying point!"

The next day Stone was commissioned a colonel of volunteers, becoming the first of some two million volunteers that would be mustered into the Union army. He was appointed Inspector General for the District of Columbia, and his first task was to examine the force available to the government in case of need. It was pitiably small. The only regulars stationed in the District were three or four hundred marines plus three officers and fifty-three enlisted men at the

Washington Arsenal. There were, however, three companies of volunteers in Washington and one in Georgetown. They were drilling, but they had not yet been taken into federal service. On New Year's Day Stone encountered at the entrance to the Metropolitan Hotel a former lieutenant in the 3rd U.S. Artillery named F.B. Schaeffer, who commanded the National Rifles, "the most fashionable militia organization in Washington." Stone stopped to chat and complimented Schaeffer on his command.

"Yes, it is a good company," said the captain, "and I suppose I shall soon have to lead it to the banks of the Susquehanna."

"Why so?"

"Why, to guard the frontier of Maryland and help keep the Yankees from coming down to coerce the South."

Stone did not tell the captain of his new appointment, but he warned him that it was imprudent to make such statements. There were other hostile units in Washington, one of which included some southern congressmen who drilled secretly almost every night in a hall over a livery stable.

Stone reported the activities of these rebel units to General Scott, but Scott warned him that he must avoid doing anything drastic. Washington was too inflammable. "We are now in such a state that a dog fight might cause the gutters to run with blood," he said.

Washington was not the only city to harbor citizens with rebellious thoughts. When Lincoln left Springfield, Illinois, for Washington on February 11, 1861, the country buzzed with ugly rumors; there was talk of plots, of traitors in government, of a *coup d'état*, and even of the assassination of Lincoln before he could take the oath of office. The prevailing sentiment in Maryland and Virginia certainly encouraged such rumors. Feeling against the president-elect appeared to be strongest in Baltimore, and Baltimore, unlike other cities through which Lincoln would pass, did not plan to give him an official reception. There would be no parade, no bands

22

playing, no speeches given there. Even the chief of police was thought to be disloyal. It seemed ominous.

Stone dispatched to Baltimore a number of detectives (on loan from the New York Metropolitan Police Force) under the direction of Detective John A. Kennedy. Unknown to Stone or to Kennedy, detectives were already in place and operating in the city; these were working for Alan Pinkerton, whose "operatives," as he called them, were, in the famous detective's words, "frequently enabled to penetrate into the abodes of crime." Pinkerton and his men had been sent to Baltimore by the president of the Philadelphia, Wilmington and Baltimore Railroad, whose concern was not for Lincoln but the protection of railroad property that violent men might damage. Both Pinkerton and Kennedy reported a plot to as-sassinate Lincoln when he passed through Baltimore. Whether both sets of detectives had uncovered the same plot or two different plots, or whether there was, in fact, any serious assassination scheme at all, has never been definitely deter-mined.

In any event, Lincoln was very reluctant to change his schedule and he tried unsuccessfully to learn whether the two warnings came from the same or independent sources. In the end he did alter his itinerary and, donning an old cloak and a soft hat as a partial disguise, he passed through Baltimore, changing from one railroad station to another undetected. Pinkerton and Stone were each convinced that he, and he alone, had saved Lincoln's life. In their separate accounts of the episode, written years afterwards, neither mentioned the other.

Fears for Lincoln's safety remained, and thus it was that swarms of troops, most of them from the volunteer companies Stone had formed, surrounded the barouche carrying Lincoln, Buchanan, Baker and Pierce to the Capitol for the inaugu-ration. And when Senator Baker stood up to introduce Lin-coln, and while Chief Justice Roger B. Taney administered the oath of office and while Lincoln delivered his inaugural address on the steps of the still domeless Capitol, there were troops all around them, including two riflemen in each window of the unfinished Capitol's wings—a precaution of Stone's.

Whether Colonel Stone did or did not save Lincoln's life, he certainly did all within his power to insure that no harm came to him in those anxious hours before and during the inauguration. He had been energetic as well in his efforts to defend the capital, for he was virtually in charge of the city's defenses. He had placed guards on all the bridges over the Potomac and on every road leading into the District. He had taken over the direction of the telegraph offices and the Baltimore Railroad; he had ordered the confiscation of ships loaded with flour bound for the South, and for the first time he had posted a guard at the White House. Mr. Lincoln and the Union were fortunate indeed to have such an officer at such a place at such a time.

Leonard Swett, an Illinois congressman close to Lincoln, spoke to Stone of the president's gratitude for all he had done and was doing. "Mr. Lincoln has no cause to be grateful to me," Stone answered. "I was opposed to his election, and believed in advance that it would bring on what is evidently coming, a fearful war. The work which I have done has not been done for him, and he need feel under no obligation to me. I have done my best toward saving the government of the country and to insure the regular inauguration of the constitutionally elected president."

This was the blunt, honest speech of a loyal soldier doing his duty, but the country was entering an era of deep suspicion, when purely political differences tended to be treated as traitorous. The days when an honest soldier could speak his mind so bluntly and still be considered loyal were fast fading, as Charles Stone was soon to discover.

2.
The Manassas Men

✳✳✳

It was early spring, the traditional season for wars to begin, and on April 12, 1861, a 10-inch mortar officially began the American Civil War when at 4:30 in the morning it opened fire on Fort Sumter in South Carolina. Lincoln immediately called for 75,000 volunteers to serve for ninety days and proclaimed a blockade of the Southern ports. Virginia, after much dithering, joined her sister states in secession, and Virginia militia seized the Norfolk Navy Yard and the arsenal at Harpers Ferry. Violence paused for breath in May; then in June a small battle was fought at Boonesville, Missouri, and George B. McClellan, leading Ohio volunteers, cleared western Virginia of most of its rebels in arms. But the eyes of the world focused on the hundred-mile-long patch of land lying between the Potomac and the James rivers. All felt that the important battles of the war would be fought in northern Virginia, and, indeed, the first one was fought on June 21 near the railway junction of Manassas along the banks of a small stream called Bull Run.

The battlefield had been selected early in May when Robert E. Lee sent Colonel Philip St. George Cocke an order "to post at Manassas Gap Junction a force sufficient to defend that point against an attack likely to be made against it by troops from Washington." Lee had clearly seen the importance of this spot, which not only included a railway junction but sat on the high road to Richmond. Cocke assembled 918 men there, but it was evident to him that this was not enough, and he advised Lee to put "a strong *corps d'armee* at Manassas." On June 1 Brigadier General Pierre G.T. Beauregard arrived and agreed with Cocke: two days later he wrote for more reinforcements. By the end of June there were six brigades strung along the banks of Bull Run, but Beauregard thought there were still not enough and he began clamoring for more.

On July 10 Miss Betty Duvall of Washington, young and beautiful, entered the Confederate lines near Fairfax and talked her way into the headquarters of Brigadier General M.L. Bonham. There she let down her long, glossy, black hair and removed from its tresses a message wrapped in a piece of black silk. It was a warning that the Union forces were about to advance. It was sent by Mrs. Rose O'Neal Greenhow, an attractive 44-year-old widow and Washington hostess. A friend of president James Buchanan and Secretary of State William Henry Seward, she nonetheless ran a Confederate spy ring from her home at 398 16th Street, N.W., a stone's throw from the White House.

In spite of this warning—passed back to Beauregard and by him to Jefferson Davis—it was not until July 17, when some Confederate outposts were attacked, that Davis whistled up more troops and sent an order to Major General Joseph E. Johnston, who had 12,000 men at Winchester, to link up with Beauregard. Johnston received the order at one o'clock on the morning of the 18th and at once began to swing his army eastward.

In Washington, neither General Scott nor Brigadier General Irvin McDowell wanted to fight—at least not just yet, not until the raw volunteers had received more training. However, many of the troops available to them had enlisted for only ninety days, and their enlistments were about to expire, and the press and public in the North were clamoring for action. Everyone wanted the war to get underway, the rhetoric to be replaced by fighting. Yielding to political pressures, Scott gave the necessary orders, and on July 16 McDowell started the first of 35,000 men down the road toward Manassas. Although the main Confederate force under Beauregard was only twenty-five miles southwest of Washington, McDowell took his time getting there, and when he finally reached the battlefield five days later, most of Johnston's army had swung down from Winchester.

The Confederate battle plan, drawn up by Beauregard and approved by Johnston, called for an attack that would turn the Union's left flank; McDowell's plan was to turn the Confederate left. The opposing armies might thus have moved in a great circle in a ponderous military ballet had they attacked simultaneously, but McDowell struck first, the opening shot coming from a Parrott 30-pounder at 5:15 on the morning of July 21 near the stone bridge over Bull Run on the Confederate left. Beauregard was taken completely by surprise. "My heart for a moment failed me," he later confessed. "I felt as though all was lost."*

McDowell's plan to send two divisions (twenty regiments of infantry plus some cavalry and artillery) around the Confederate left flank was a good one, and with better-trained troops and a little luck he might have made himself a hero and shortened the war. Perhaps all he really needed was luck, for the Southern troops were as raw and untrained as his own. But McDowell was unlucky. Defending the stone bridge was a Confederate commander who possessed all the qualities needed that day to spoil his battle plan and save the day for the Confederates, turning probable defeat into a splendid victory. His name was Lieutenant Colonel Nathan Evans.

Evans's command that day was a patchwork of fourteen companies and two 6-pounder howitzers on the extreme left of the Confederate line. By 8:00 A.M. Evans's sharp eyes and

---

*From a letter to Miss Augusta Evans in Mobile, Alabama, March 24, 1863.

quick brain had convinced him that the force attacking him was not the main thrust. Forty-five minutes later a Confederate signal officer, Captain (later Brigadier General) E. Porter Alexander, standing on a high observation point within the defenses, caught the flash of sunlight off a Union artillery tube on Evans's left front. Adjusting his glasses, he looked close and saw the glistening bayonets moving through the trees. He at once "wig-wagged" with a signal flag to Evans: "Look out to your left. You are turned." *

Evans did not hesitate or ask for orders. Leaving only four companies to guard the bridge, he marched the bulk of his command about 1,700 yards northwards and at about 10:15 A.M. opened fire on the advancing Federal column, Colonel Ambrose E. Burnside's brigade. For a few minutes the Federals were stopped, but they possessed overwhelming force, and Evans called on Brigadier General Barnard S. Bee to come to his support. Bee, who commanded his own brigade plus two Georgia regiments, responded promptly. By 11:00 A.M. he had moved his troops into line on Evans's right. For an hour this force, consisting of the equivalent of about six regiments with six field pieces, held back the Union army's main thrust. But the Federals brought up reinforcements, and the Confederates fell back in considerable confusion. Just then Thomas Jackson's brigade, which had just come up, moved into a firm position on Henry Hill. It was then that Bee, frantically attempting to control his near-demoralized men, leaned forward in his stirrups, pointed with his sword, and called out, "Look! There is Jackson standing like a stone wall! Rally behind the Virginians!" Bee was referring to Jackson's brigade, but the sobriquet "Stonewall" clung to its commander.

The battle raged into the hot summer's afternoon. It was, as Wellington said of Waterloo, "a near run thing," but at

---

*This is the first recorded instance of this signaling system being used in combat.

28

last the Union forces broke and fled back, a disorderly mob, towards Washington. Washington and the North wailed in despair; Richmond and the South exalted and succumbed to the sin of pride and a dangerous overconfidence in the abilities of Southern soldiers. Of the Federal army of 35,000 men, 2,896 were lost—killed, wounded, captured or missing; of the Confederate army of 32,000 men, 1,982 were lost. The battle had proven, among other things, that the war was not to be a picnic. In fact, Alfred Ely, congressman from Rochester, New York, and several other civilians who brought their picnic baskets along when they journeyed out from Washington to watch the battle, ended up in Confederate prisons; luckier picnickers scurried back to the capital, a basic lesson of war well learned.

At First Manassas, or First Bull Run, 67,000 amateur soldiers began their military education. This was not the way men were supposed to be educated, for the examination preceded their study of the subject, but a battle concentrates the mind wonderfully, and some of the soldiers proved to be fast learners. The fates loyal to Mars decreed that there were to be more fast learners among the Confederate officers than among the Union officers, and no less than forty-two colonels and officers of lesser rank in the rebel ranks that day rose to become general officers. These came to be called the "Manassas men." Ten of them—nearly a quarter—were to win their stars but lose their lives before the war ended. Jubal A. Early, James E.B. ("Jeb") Stuart, Sidney Longstreet, Rob Wheat and Wade Hampton were all Manassas Men, and so too was 37-year-old Nathan George Evans.

No single man had done more to convert the battle at Manassas into a victory than Evans. His quick action and bold leadership had prevented McDowell's great flanking attack from achieving the success it might well have attained. Historians seem to have agreed that McDowell failed at Bull Run because he planned an attack that was too complicated for his untrained troops to execute, a conclusion that deserves re-examination. Had a man less quick and bold than Evans been in command of the Confederates at the stone bridge, history's verdict might have been that McDowell's battle plan was brilliant. In the after-action reports of his superiors, Evans was praised for his "Dauntless conduct and imperturbable coolness," and for his "skill and unshakable courage." He was promoted to colonel, but history has recorded his achievements without comment; his superiors did not mark him as a man to watch.

Nathan Evans was of medium height; he was growing bald, but he possessed a great black mustache and "small, restless eyes." His nickname was "Shanks," given him at West Point, for his legs were thin and, according to some, knock-kneed. He was shrewd—some said cunning—and he was thought contentious, but he appears to have been scarcely more so than the average senior officer in the Civil War, for they were, North and South, a contentious lot. Fitzhugh Lee called Evans a "riproaring, scorn-all-care" type—and he drank, many thought to excess. Although a good soldier, he was never popular with his officers or men.

Evans was born in Marion, South Carolina. After attending Randolph-Macon College for a spell, he entered West Point and was graduated in 1848, standing 36th out of a class of 38. Upon graduation he served with cavalry regiments in the Far West, and, prior to resigning his commission five months before Bull Run and accepting a commission as a major in the army of his native South Carolina, he had been a captain in the 2nd United States Cavalry.

At First Manassas Evans had shown that he possessed not only personal courage, but leadership and tactical abilities of a high order. In short, he had those qualities which Lee, ever searching for capable leadership, might have discovered; he might have been selected for high command. But it was Jackson, thanks to Bee's apposite simile, whose fame was firmly

In some respects Confederate Colonel Nathan G. Evans resembled Ulysses S. Grant. Like the Union general, in spite of being graduated near the bottom of his class at West Point and earning a reputation as a drinker, Evans was nonetheless a shrewd and decisive leader in battle. His tactical skill served him well at Ball's Bluff.

founded at Bull Run. It is "Stonewall" Jackson's statue that today dominates the manicured battlefield; there is no statue to "Shanks" Evans.

Eppa Hunton, thirty-nine years old and commanding the 8th Virginia, was another Manassas Man. Although he had not had an opportunity to distinguish himself at Bull Run, he had "borne himself gallantly." This was his first fight, but not his last. Few officers and few regiments, North or South, were to fight in as many battles as Hunton and the 8th Virginia. The regiment came to be called, with much reason, the "Bloody Eighth." All were recruited in northern Virginia: six of the ten companies came from Loudoun County, in and around Leesburg, and the remaining companies from neighboring counties.

Hunton aspired to a high moral code, and the three sins against which he constantly preached were smoking, drinking and gambling. He did not, of course, approve of hard-drinking Shanks Evans, under whom he was about to serve. He was a brave man who loved his regiment; he took care of his men and personally led them into battle. Of First Manassas he said, "I felt very proud of my dear boys, and believe they felt proud of me. I hope so." He was openly sentimental and often spoke of his soldiers as "my brave boys" or "dear boys", and he spoke of his wife as "my dear wife"; after the war he often spoke of "our dear lost cause."

He was from the beginning a secessionist, and he thought Abraham Lincoln "one of the most vulgar men that ever attained high position in the United States." As a delegate to the Virginia Secession Convention he had fretted over the lengthy debate that preceded the signing of the Ordinance of Secession. When Virginia mobilized, he resigned a commission as a brigadier general in the militia and sought an active command. He was delighted to be elected colonel of the 8th Virginia.

Another Manassas Man was 40-year-old William Barksdale.

He was a quarrelsome man, but a good soldier, noted for his coolness under fire; in desperate situations, he did not panic. He was born in Tennessee in 1821 and after attending the University of Nashville and studying law in Columbus, Mississippi, he became editor of the Columbus *Democrat*, a violently pro-slavery newspaper. He served in the Mexican War and rose from private to captain. From 1853 until 1861 he was a member of Congress, but with war in the wind, he returned to Mississippi and was appointed quartermaster-general of the Mississippi Army. However, like all officers who longed for active service, he wanted a regiment and was pleased when he was elected colonel of the 13th Mississippi.

Barksdale had a fine regiment of volunteers, but he had some trouble getting it to the Manassas battlefield intact. The chorus of the "Song of the Mississippi Volunteers," a popular tune, at least in Mississippi ran:

> *We go walking on the green grass thus, thus, thus.*
> *Come all ye fair and pretty maids and walk along*
> *   with us.*
> *So pretty and fair as you take yourselves to be,*
> *I'll choose you for a partner, come along with me.*

It would appear that many a fair and pretty girl did take a walk with a bold Mississippi volunteer and was chosen as a partner of sorts, but unfortunately not all the girls were maids. In Richmond on July 11, 1861, Barksdale reported that he had a great deal of sickness in his regiment, mostly from measles and what he described as the result of "improper sexual indulgence." The following month the 18th Mississippi, with whom the 13th was soon to be brigaded, reported twenty-five new cases of gonorrhea.

For commanding officers, venereal diseases were a problem: more soldiers were to be struck down by Venus than by Mars in this war. Complete statistics are not available for the Confederates, but on the Union side, one out of every twelve soldiers contracted a venereal disease in just the first year of the war, and probably the ratio was comparable for the Southern armies. Units such as the 13th and 18th Mississippi, composed mostly of farm boys who had never been far from home, seemed to be particularly vulnerable when passing through metropolitan areas.

Another Mississippi regiment that fought at First Manassas was the 17th. In April of 1861 its Company G was raised in Holly Springs, then a town of 5,000 people boasting four colleges. The company called itself the Confederate Guards, and its 150 members included 97 farmers, 20 students, 8 "railroaders", 4 clerks, 3 carpenters, 3 schoolteachers, 2 doctors, 2 merchants, a harness maker, a gin maker, a wheelwright, a joiner, a painter, a printer and a lawyer. One in seven was married. (Not many survived the war unscathed; two-thirds did not return at all. More than half were wounded, 30 were killed or died of wounds, 68 died of diseases and one deserted.)

The lawyer in Company G was W.S. (for Winfield Scott) Featherston, forty-two, who was at once elected captain and two months later was elected colonel of the regiment. Like Barksdale, Featherston was born in Tennessee, migrated to Mississippi, was admitted to the bar, and served in Congress. His only military experience had been as a volunteer in the war against the Creek Indians in 1836, but he had a commanding presence, and on both sides in the war, successful political experience was inferred to be proof of latent military abilities. He stood more than six feet tall, was clean shaven and sharp featured. His formal education was exiguous and his manner blunt. He was careless of his appearance, but he developed a reputation for hard drill. Private Frank Moore, who served under him, said: "The boys all think a good deal of him; although he is slow, he is a very good officer and as brave and cool a man as ever went on a battle field."

After First Manassas these four Manassas Men—Evans, Hunton, Featherston and Barksdale—were joined by Colonel E.R. Burt and the 18th Mississippi (mean strength 975 men) and sent to the northern Virginia piedmont area, to Loudoun County. The 13th, 17th and 18th Mississippi and the 8th Virginia were supplemented by three companies of Virginia cavalry and by 1st Company, Richmond Howitzers. This brigade was under the command of Nathan "Shanks" Evans.

The 1st Richmond Howitzers was composed of men who were more educated than those found in most military units of the day. Many had attended college and most were businessmen or clerks from Richmond. The battery had a glee club and a "law club"; one man kept a diary in Greek. Robert Stiles, a recent Yale graduate who enlisted, wrote: "Few things have impressed me as did the intellectual and moral character of the men who composed the circle I entered. . . . Around the camp fires of the First Company, Richmond Howitzers, I found throbbing an intellectual life as high and brilliant and intense as any I had ever known." He found striking the differences between his companions and the men in the Mississippi regiments, "bear hunters from the swamps and cane breaks and, naturally enough, almost without exception fine shots. . . . At times they seemed almost as rough as the bears they hunted, yet they were withal simple-minded and tender-hearted boys."

The Virginia cavalry was under the command of 38-year-old Lieutenant Colonel Walter H. Jenifer. He had entered West Point in 1841 in the same class as Charles Stone, but he had lasted less than seven months as a cadet. Nevertheless, in 1847 he was commissioned a second lieutenant and posted to the 2nd Cavalry, the same unit to which Evans, two years later, was also assigned as a second lieutenant. On March 3, 1855, both Jenifer and Evans were promoted to first lieutenant in the same regiment. Jenifer made a name for himself as a horse trainer and the designer of a saddle that was widely used in the army until superceded by the saddle designed by George McClellan. But he was still only a first lieutenant when on April 30, 1861, he resigned his commission to join the Confederate army.

During the war Jenifer rode a magnificent Arabian stallion that was noted for its intelligence, so superbly trained that, as one officer said, "it was hard to imagine anything a horse could do which this one would not do at Jenifer's command." There were some who admired the horse more than its master. General George Crittenden watched Jenifer ride by one day and remarked to Captain John Haskell: "There is Jenifer with his horse that has more sense than he has, for Jenifer has taught him everything he ever knew, and he had a lot of horse-sense to begin with."

The four infantry regiments, the battery and the cavalry, the 7th Brigade in General Pierre Beauregard's I Corps of the Confederate Army of the Potomac, assembled in beautiful Loudoun County, its valleys dotted with stone cottages and log cabins: the Mississippi volunteers so far from home, the bright young men from Richmond, and the men of the 8th Virginia, for whom the county was familiar country.

3.
On the Upper Potomac

Leesburg, Virginia, county seat of Loudoun, lies just east of the Catoctin range of low, rounded mountains (called Hogback south of Leesburg) that run north and south, roughly paralleling the Potomac, which flows northwest to southeast, down to Washington and beyond, emptying into Chesapeake Bay. Around Leesburg, in the four or five miles between the Catoctin mountains and the Potomac, the land is softly rolling until about a quarter of a mile from the river where its character changes abruptly, the placid farmland turning to woods amid an eruption of hills and deep ravines, ending along the river in cliffs a hundred feet high. Ball's Bluff this area is called. From the top of the bluff one can look across a narrow stretch of the river to Harrison's Island, 500 acres of flat, wood-fringed farmland shaped like a huge dolphin caught in the Potomac, a great stationary fish in a river too small for it to move. About twenty-five miles upstream, where the Shenandoah joins the Potomac, is Harpers Ferry, made famous when, two years before, John Brown had tried to raid the federal arsenal there and spark a slave insurrection.

Between Great Falls, just above Washington, and Harpers Ferry there was, or had been, a bridge at Berlin (now Brunswick, Maryland), but Confederate cavalry had burned it down one Sunday in June 1861. There were, however, other places to cross the river. The first crossing downstream was Noland's

Ferry, near the mouth of the Monocacy River; nearby was Spink's Ferry and, about three miles further down, White's Ford, though this was little used; another three miles downstream, near the northern tip of Harrison's island, was Conrad's Ferry (now called White's Ferry, and the only ferry still operating on the Potomac). Five miles below was Edwards Ferry. In what is now northwestern Virginia the Potomac was the boundary between the Union and the Confederacy. Both sides had troops guarding its shores.

Evans's brigade was an outpost on the left flank of Beauregard's army; its assigned task in Loudoun was to keep a sharp eye on the river, particularly its fords and ferries, and a weather eye on the turnpike that linked Leesburg with Alexandria. About two miles east of Leesburg Evans threw up some substantial earthworks, enclosing about an acre and a half, which he called Fort Evans,* and it was here that he established his headquarters. Pickets and outposts were set up along the Virginia shore and down the turnpike. General R.W. Wright, who commanded the Loudoun Militia, lived about eight miles away, and it was thought that he could be called on to muster his men should the need arise.

Nearby Leesburg was a pleasant, comfortable town of three or four thousand people, and Loudoun County in the early autumn presented—as it still does—as fair and peaceful a landscape as one is ever likely to find. Being a border county, the ragged, uneven line that divided Northern and Southern sentiments ran through it. But most of the Union sympathizers, those who, in the words of the Leesburg *Democrat*, had "bartered their birth-right for a miserable mess of Federal porridge," together with the neutral Quakers, lived on the western side of the Catoctin range, around Waterford and Lovettsville. Leesburg and its immediate environs was pretty

---

*The fort is still extant, as are some Confederate trenches. They are on private property.

solidly for the South, and it opened its arms in welcome to the men of Evans's brigade. Robert Stiles of the Richmond Howitzers later wrote: "Leesburg . . . was at this time, perhaps, the most desirable post in our lives, on account of the character both of the country and its people . . . the latter whole-hearted and hospitable, ready to share with us all they had. If ever soldiers had a more ideal time than we enjoyed at Leesburg, then I cannot conceive when or where it was." Private Robert A. Moore of the 17th Mississippi wrote in his diary on October 10: "I think Leesburg can boast of as fair daughters as any other town in the state. The boys are very merry, some of them have a dance nearly every night, & others go to prayer-meeting."

Although Federal troops were just across the river, most of the citizens of Loudoun County were too interested in the upcoming elections for the presidency and vice presidency of the Confederate States of America to worry much about a Union attack. There was no sense of impending danger, only the excitement of creating a new nation. Fears for the future were smothered by an unbounded confidence in the superiority of Confederate arms.

Across the Potomac on the Maryland side was Charles P. Stone, who had risen rapidly as a result of his efficient work in the defense of Washington and its government. When the Congress authorized additional regiments for the regular army, he had been given command of the newly formed 14th Infantry, and on May 14 he was made a colonel in the regular army, leaping over the heads of a considerable number of older officers, including his father-in-law, Robert E. Clary, a lieutenant colonel in the Quartermaster Corps, who had served continuously in the army since his graduation from West Point in 1828.

Stone never took command of his regiment, for just three days later he was appointed a brigadier general of volunteers, and not long after was appointed to a major general's command: an infantry division. His unit was called a Corps of Observation, and his task, like that of Evans, was to watch the river between Point of Rocks (ten miles north of Leesburg) and Edwards Ferry. Up river, to guard the shore between Point of Rocks and Harpers Ferry, was a regiment under Colonel John W. Geary which did not come under Stone's command; downstream, guarding the river between Edwards Ferry and Washington, was a full division under Major General Nathaniel Banks; directly across from Washington on the Virginia side of the river were two divisions under generals W.F. Smith and George A. McCall. Such were McClellan's dispositions for the defense of Washington and Maryland.

Stone and Evans, the opposing commanders on the upper Potomac, were the same age and, although not in the same class at West Point, they had been there together for a year and they knew each other. Both were professional soldiers, but their temperaments were as different as Grant's and Lee's. Curiously, Stone's personality resembled in some ways that of Lee, while Evans most resembled Grant.

The words "accomplished gentleman" were most often used by friends and enemies alike to characterize Stone. He had a certain reticence; he thought before he spoke and tried to choose his words carefully. He was courteous, chivalrous even, and he had beautiful manners. But his gentlemanliness went beyond mere politeness, and he possessed "a keen sense of honor." He was methodical and orderly; in the administration of his division he exhibited a standard of excellence not often found in Civil War units at this date. The historian of the 20th Massachusetts recorded that "General Stone was a most active, vigilant officer, visiting his camps at all hours of the day and night, thoroughly inspecting the troops and attending to all the details of camp life. No officer or guard would dare sleep or neglect his duty, for General Stone might appear at any moment."

But Stone was more admired than loved. The handful of

professional officers and those volunteers who took their soldiering seriously respected him, but some of the militia and volunteer officers thought his standards too high and his discipline too strict. With his Van Dyck beard and drooping mustaches, his ramrod straight back and aristocratic manners, Stone was not the sort of person to whom the Minnesota lumber jacks, Massachusetts fishermen or the young men from New York's boroughs could take an instant liking; he was not the popular sort that Pennsylvania farm boys would elect captain of their militia company. There was a fire in Charles Stone, but it was seldom visible to the world. Henry Foote, quartermaster of the 2nd New York State Militia, said that he was "not a man that gets a particular hold of the hearts and enthusiasm of volunteer soldiers."

Perhaps Stone was a general in the wrong era or in the wrong country. There prevailed a greater spirit of independence in the land then: men spoke their minds more freely, they judged more quickly, acted more impetuously and had less regard for the legally constituted authorities. The soldiers, from farms and small towns mostly, came equipped with simple creeds deeply felt: they were young men who were easy to lead but hard to drive. They responded eagerly to words that touched their emotions, for they were sentimental, but sullenly to the formal words of command and to official orders. In an army of professionals, or in a royal army officered by aristocrats, Stone might have been an outstanding general; in an army of republican, independent-minded citizens, he lacked that coarse streak of bravado that men in ill-disciplined masses require of their leaders. He would have made a poor politician—at least a poor American politician—for he lacked the ready smile, the bonhomie, the flashiness that make a man a popular leader.

Stone never felt the need to explain himself, his orders or his actions, to those whom he thought had no need to know. In an inquisitive and gossipy army of amateurs, he was often

41

misunderstood. This is not to say that he was overbearing, condescending, rude to inferiors, or that he possessed any of the other faults sometimes associated with those whose wealth, power, education or social position place them above the common man. It was simply that his manners were formal and his personality, following his temperament, tended to be more aristocratic than democratic.

None of Stone's troops—young men from Massachusetts, Michigan, Minnesota, Pennsylvania and New York—were professional soldiers; most had been in the army but a few weeks and few of their officers knew more than their men about soldiering. None had yet seen action, although Baker's California Regiment had received its baptism of fire—not from the Confederates, but from the 4th Michigan, which on September 28 had fired on it by mistake, killing four and wounding fourteen. Many of the soldiers were mere boys. How many is unknown, but 846,000 boys under the age of eighteen were eventually to serve in the Union army and their enlistment was often encouraged. In Philadelphia, where most of the California Regiment was recruited, any boy in the highest grade of high school who enlisted was entitled to graduate with his class.

They were all eager for war, these first volunteers, and they had been given an enthusiastic send-off when they left home. Jasper Searles in a letter home described the reception given the 1st Minnesota as by boat, train and foot it made its way to the seat of war: "All along the road through Wis., Ill., Ind., Ohio, Penn., Md., we were cheered from almost every home. The boys tired themselves more from yelling than from anything they had to perform. . . . At every station we found old men and women ready to greet us . . . and in one instance an old lady, gray headed and trembling, sat in her door as we passed and blessed us in words and actions so fervently that she resembled a spiritual medium through her gyrations."

These cheering young men of the 1st Minnesota, 1,042

strong and uniformed in cherry red woolen shirts and black pants, were on their way to a bloodbath. By the time the regiment reached Gettysburg in 1863 it was down to 262 officers and men; on the second day of the battle 215 of these were casualties—the highest loss sustained by a regiment in proportion to the numbers engaged in modern history.

In the early days of the war, trains packed with cheering troops were part of the landscape. All accounts of soldiers setting off to war speak of their cheering. William Howard Russell, the famous British war correspondent who had made his reputation in the Crimean War, was crossing Maryland early in October, and he too observed the phenomena. In his dispatches to *The Times* he wrote of "monster trains . . . and the soldiers inside rend the air with yells and shrill cheers."

For the 1st Minnesota, as for the Tammany Regiment, the California Regiment, the 15th and 20th Massachusetts, the road to war led at first only to Stone's Corps of Observation in the quiet Maryland countryside along the Potomac where their days were spent, not in the smoke of battle, but learning the elements of soldiering and the routine of camp life, or leaning on their muskets and watching the wooded Virginia shore and the rolling waters of the river. It was perhaps thoughts of such duty that led Justice Oliver Wendell Holmes, Jr., to describe war as an "organized bore."

But there was need for training. Colonel William R. Lee of the 20th Massachusetts discovered that his city-bred young men from Boston and his fishermen from Nantucket did not know how to shoot. When their grandfathers and great grand-fathers had taken down their muskets to oppose the British redcoats, they had handled their weapons expertly with easy familiarity: their descendants were inclined to close their eyes and jerk the trigger.

It was difficult for most volunteers to understand military discipline. It was, for example, standard practice in the United States Army at the time—and indeed remained so until World

War II—for members of the regimental band to serve as
stretcher bearers in combat. It made sense: there was little
use for stretcher bearers until there was a fight, and there was
no use for a band in battle; the same men could perform the
two dissimilar functions. But the bandsmen of the 15th Massachusetts did not understand this reasoning, or chose not
to. They protested vehemently when ordered to spend one
hour a day learning to apply a tourniquet, to press an artery,
or to carry a wounded man. They refused to turn out for the
drill and announced haughtily that they would rather die than
do such menial work. Their colonel, Charles Devens, a 41-
year-old Massachusetts lawyer and politician, was said to possess an "urbane and kindly nature," but he refused to put up
with insubordination; he promptly confined the lot, and told
them they would get food when they decided to do their duty.
None starved. However, soon after, when their services as
medics were required in earnest, they balked once more.

Colonel Devens was a handsome man and a patrician. He
had attended the Boston Latin School and had been graduated
from Harvard in 1838. Two years later he was admitted to
the bar. He had been for three years the city solicitor for
Worcester, he had served two terms in the Massachusetts state
legislature, and he was for four years a United States Marshal
for the district of Massachusetts, a position that sometimes
involved duties conflicting with his strong anti-slavery sentiments.

Under the Fugitive Slave Act of 1850, runaway slaves when
caught were placed under the jurisdiction of the federal government, and claims for them were heard by a federal commissioner. The slaves themselves, being considered property,
were not allowed to testify. If the commissioner ruled that
the slave was not the property of the person claiming him,
the commissioner's fee was reduced by half. There had been
attempts to repeal the law, and its constitutionality had been
questioned, but only a year before the southern states seceded,

the Supreme Court had declared it to be constitutional. Lincoln favored it, or at least he was not against it, and in a speech just before his election he said, "I do not now, nor ever did, stand in favor of the unconditional repeal of the Fugitive Slave Law."

The law placed upon the federal government the responsibility for returning runaway slaves at government expense. When an escaped slave named Sims from Savannah was arrested in Boston and the United States commissioner who heard his case decided in favor of the claimed owner, Devens, as United States Marshal, was ordered to return Sims to Savannah. It was a distasteful errand. Four years later he tried unsuccessfully to buy Sims' freedom. When through the fortunes of war Sims was liberated, Devens exerted himself to find a government job for him.

Devens was to survive the war, though severely wounded at Fair Oaks and again at Chancellorsville; at Cold Harbor he was so crippled by inflammatory rheumatism that he had to be carried onto the battlefield. He emerged a major general, became a judge of the Massachusetts Supreme Court, and then Attorney General in president Rutherford B. Hayes's cabinet.

Devens was not alone in his abolitionist sentiments; they were shared by most of the Massachusetts troops. Men from Michigan and Minnesota who had joined the army to preserve the Union sometimes jeered at the abolitionist Massachusetts men who had joined to strike a blow against slavery. John Albion Andrew, the 40-year-old governor of Massachusetts, was one of the foremost anti-slavery politicians in the country; one of his enthusiastic admirers called him "the most Christ-like of all war's ministers." He had spoken in defense of John Brown and believed that slaves could only win their freedom by force of arms. A short, heavy man with dark, curly hair and a dimpled chin, he was one of the first to believe that a civil war was inevitable and that the federal government and the northern states ought to prepare for it. Immediately after his inauguration in January 1861 he dispatched a man to England to buy Enfield rifles; he called up the militia and expended his tremendous energy in rousing the state legislature to provide for them, which they did: the troops from Massachusetts were to be the best clothed and equipped troops in the Union army.

During the frantic preparations for war, Governor Andrew's office was crowded with supplicants for commissions, contracts and permissions of all sorts, as well as people offering goods and services. Horace Binney Sargent has given us a picture of some of them:

> There were . . . inventors of new-fangled guns, pistols and sabres, only dangerous to their possessors, and which the inventors, to our great joy, threatened to sell to the Confederacy if we did not buy them; gentlemen far gone with consumption, desiring gentle horseback experience in the cavalry . . . saddlers, proposing sole-leather cuirasses shaped like the tip of a coffin; bands of sweet-eyed, blushing girls, bringing in nice long nightgowns "for the poor soldiers," or more imaginative garments, "fearfully and wonderfully made," redolent of patriotism and innocence, embroidered with the Stars and Stripes, and too big for Goliath.

The sense of urgency felt in Massachusetts was in striking contrast to the attitudes exhibited elsewhere in the North. The nation was indeed on the brink of war, but in the Michigan state legislature a proposal to raise two new militia regiments dissolved the lawmakers in laughter and buffoonery when a wag questioned the meaning of the term "field officer," and someone suggested that "corn field officer" would be more appropriate. Then, as now, lawmakers were easily amused.

In Massachusetts too there were jokes, but Governor Andrew remained deadly serious. He was determined to provide good warm overcoats for the Massachusetts troops, and he talked about overcoats so much that people began to laugh at him; "overcoat" became a slang term for those who thought a civil war inevitable. But when the war started and on a cold, sleety day the Massachusetts regiments began to assemble in Boston, the young soldiers and their mothers had reason to be grateful for the foresight of their governor.

The overcoats were not only warm, they were handsome. Blue and grey were not yet the colors which distinguished the opposing armies, and the overcoats of the Massachusetts infantry were grey with scarlet linings. When the 20th Massachusetts reached the banks of the Potomac, General Stone inquired of Colonel Lee if the men had all the clothing and equipment they required. "My regiment, sir," said Lee proudly, "came from Massachusetts!"

When Lincoln issued his urgent appeal for 75,000 men, Massachusetts had been quick to respond; volunteers had already been formed into regiments and most were ready to march. There had even been some discussion as to how they could be sent to Washington, for if they went overland they would have to pass through hostile Maryland. Most thought it would be better if the troops went by sea, but when Andrew asked Washington how the troops should proceed, the answer came back: "Send them by rail." So off went five regiments of infantry, clothed and completely equipped at the state's expense, and the state's first casualties were suffered when the 6th Massachusetts was stoned and fired on while moving from one railway station to another in Baltimore. Several sets of casualty figures exist, but it would appear that about four men were killed and forty wounded.

To form his regiments, Andrew had need of more than clothing and equipment. The state's youth eagerly responded to his call for men, but officers to train them were few. There was no lack of applications, and the field officers were quickly chosen from among former officers and politicians, but Andrew was at a loss as to how to select the junior officers from among the many young men who applied for commissions. On his staff, however, was Harry Lee, a handsome, witty Harvard graduate and noted financier. "Leave this to me," he told Andrew. "I don't know all these boys, but I've known most of their fathers or uncles or grandfathers. Here, this young fellow's grandfather was a first-rate captain at Louisburg. Why isn't that as good a yardstick as anything?" Andrew agreed and turned the selection of junior officers over to Harry Lee.

So on the basis of family histories commissions were handed out—family histories and education. Harvard graduates were never refused commissions. Lee reasoned that if they did not know anything about military service or war, they had the capacity to learn. Thus, Oliver Wendell Holmes, Jr., age 20, son of a famous father ("The autocrat of the breakfast table") and a nephew of Harry Lee, received a commission as a first lieutenant in Company A of the 20th Massachusetts Volunteer Infantry six days after his graduation from Harvard in July 1861.* In October he found himself with his regiment, part of Frederick W. Lander's brigade, camped in a wheat field a mile and a half northeast of Edwards Ferry.

Young Holmes found the 20th Massachusetts filled with friends, relatives and other Harvard graduates. So many of the officers were Harvard men that the regiment was sometimes called the Harvard Regiment. In it were Lieutenant Colonel Francis W. Palfrey (Harvard '51); Surgeon Henry Bryant (Harvard '40): Second Lieutenant Henry Livermore Abbott (Harvard '60); First Lieutenant James Lowell (Harvard

---

*Holmes was one of seven future justices of the Supreme Court who fought in the Civil War: John M. Harlan, William B. Woods and Stanley Mathews fought for the Union; Edward D. White, Horace H. Luston and Lucius Q. Lamar fought for the Confederacy.

'58), a cousin of young Holmes and a nephew of James Russell Lowell, the poet; and Holmes's cousin and former classmate, Second Lieutenant William Lowell Putnam, a brother-in-law of James Russell Lowell. Putnam, golden-haired, hazel-eyed, tall and straight, had been considered the "handsomest man at Harvard College." The major of the regiment was Paul Joseph Revere (Harvard '52) who, like his brother, Surgeon Edward H.R. Revere (Harvard Medical School '49), was a grandson of the famous rider in the night. Captain William Francis Bartlett, tall and slender, who was to become one of his regiment's heroes, had been a junior at Harvard when the war started but left to join the fight.

William Raymond Lee, a civil engineer and railway superintendent, was the regiment's colonel. He was not a Harvard man, but he had attended the United States Military Academy at West Point, entering with the class of 1829. He did not graduate, however, for just two weeks before graduation his father had a "brain attack" and disappeared; Lee resigned to look for him. A classmate and one of his intimate friends was Robert E. Lee; he also knew Jefferson Davis, who had been in the class just ahead of his. At fifty-seven Lee was said to be the oldest colonel in the Army of the Potomac. He had led an adventurous life, having survived a shipwreck in the Gulf of Mexico and a year's confinement by the Mexican authorities. During Mackenzie's Rebellion in Ontario (1837-38) he had been sent to Canada by the American government to report on events there; he performed a similar service during the "Florida War." When superintendent of the Boston and Providence Railroad, he had been the first railroad man to burn coal instead of wood in his engines.

Before they left their native state the 20th Massachusetts had been presented with a fine regimental flag of white silk made by the patriotic ladies of Boston. On one side was worked the arms of the commonwealth and on the other the words *Fide et Constantia*. Two companies, including Holmes's Com-

49

pany A, had been equipped with the fine Enfield rifles Governor Andrew had ordered from England. The men armed with them were proud indeed of their weapons; the rest of the companies had only old smoothbore muskets.

In the beginning, the 20th Massachusetts was not a completely happy regiment. As Colonel William Lee put it, "The regiment . . . had in it elements which required strong and judicious government." Unlike the 15th and other Massachusetts regiments then formed, the 20th did not come from one town or county. Although all came from the same state, there were considerable differences—between farmers and fishermen, between Bostonians and those from small towns and villages, between old, established families and immigrants—and they clashed. Even among the officers there was friction between those who had been educated at Harvard and those who had not.

There were two companies of Germans in the regiment. Their commanding officers were older than most of the other captains; they were of foreign birth and they had not attended Harvard: Captain Ferdinance Dreher, thirty-nine, of Boston, commanded Company C, and Captain John Herchenroder, thirty-one, also of Boston, commanded Company B. Company E was partly composed of Germans; its commanding officer was George Adam Schmitt, thirty-four, who had been a German instructor at Harvard and was the only member of the Harvard faculty to enlist during the war. Dreher, who had been an officer in the German army, was later to write to Governor Andrew (volunteer officers on both sides often wrote their state governors) saying that "the regiment was officered by young men, belonging to a certain aristocratic clique. Not only we German officers in the Regiment were made to feel it, there is Captain Allen Shepard and Lieut. James Murphy." Dreher mentioned that Holmes was one of the members of the clique, and he gave Andrew his opinion of the lot: "I would take all the military science of this (sic) gentlemen and put them in a private, and it would *not make* the best sergeant we have." There must have been something to Dreher's complaint, for Devens (Harvard '38) himself an aristocrat, told Palfrey that "the sooner you get this blue-blood notion out of your head the better for yourself and the regiment." However, by the end of the war no fewer than nine officers of the regiment, all "blue-bloods," reached general officer rank; three of these—including George Macy, whom Dreher had named as one of the leaders of the clique—became major generals.

The diversity of occupation among the troops was evident in Company A, Lieutenant Holmes's company, which came from all parts of the state. It included at least one laborer, farmer, sailor, carpenter, hostler, shoemaker, iron worker, cooper, nailer, tailor, brickmaker, teamster, hatter, silversmith—and Private Daniel Ford, whose occupation was melodeon maker. The company's first sergeant was Harry J. Smith, twenty-three, an artist from Salem. He was not a success, for shortly after the battle of Ball's Bluff he was demoted to private and in May 1862, he deserted.

The 20th Massachusetts, being a somewhat peculiar regiment, had experienced some difficulty in recruiting, and it was understrength when it arrived on the upper Potomac, mustering only 650 muskets. The 15th Massachusetts, on the other hand, was a full strength regiment; a high percentage of its men were descendants of men who had fought in the Revolutionary War, and it had been recruited from one county: Worcester. Its companies were more commonly called by the names of the towns from which its men were recruited; thus, Company B was called the Fitchburg Company, Company G was the Grafton Company, and Company H was the Northbridge Company. When the ladies of Fitchburg presented Company B with a flag, Captain (soon after major) John Kimball made his men take an oath that "it should never trail in the dust while a single arm was left to uphold it."

It was not until July 26 that the 15th received its full complement of muskets. Companies A and C were armed with what were called Harpers Ferry rifles—rifled muskets using percussion caps—while the rest were issued old smooth-bores that had been altered to take percussion caps. Some of the latter were so badly worn that they were unfit for service.

On August 7 an elaborate ceremony at the Worcester city hall included speeches, prayers and the presentation of a regimental flag made by women in the county. The event culminated with the band playing "Hail Columbia" while a sergeant on the platform waved the flag to and fro. Filled with patriotic fervor, "the ladies sprang to their feet and waved their handkerchieves, while cheers, loud and hearty, went up for the colors of the Fifteenth Regiment." At six o'clock the next morning the regiment, 1,046 officers and men, set off for the war.

Like all Massachusetts regiments, the 15th was nervous when it arrived in Baltimore, for all knew of the attacks by a mob on the 6th Massachusetts here four months earlier, and it, too, faced the mile-long march from one depot to another. When they had detrained, Colonel Devens gave the order for his men to load their weapons. This caused a stir among the spectators, followed by a stampede when one of the muskets accidentally discharged.

Actually, there was no need for Devens to be concerned. Another Massachusetts lawyer-politician turned soldier, Major General Benjamin Butler, had laid a heavy hand on eastern Maryland and made it safe for Union volunteers. He had arrested the mayor of Baltimore, nineteen state legislators and a number of other prominent citizens who had expressed their objections to the war. Secessionist sentiment had cooled considerably, and the 15th Massachusetts was actually cheered. In fact, said one soldier, "Jeff Davis was not mentioned except by a few boys." One old man stepped out of the crowd to ask John Kimball what regiment was passing; when told, he took off his hat and cried, "God bless the grand old state of Massachusetts!"

In camp on the Potomac the Massachusetts soldiers proved that while they did not yet know how to shoot, they still possessed yankee ingenuity. The 20th Massachusetts constructed ovens to bake fresh bread—an improvement over the issue hardtack—and they were so proud of their accomplishment that they sent six loaves to Governor Andrew. No other regiment had fresh bread, they boasted, but they were mistaken. Their neighbors on the upper Potomac, the 1st Minnesota, which contained several companies of lumberjacks, were equally ingenious, and they too had bake ovens.

Stone's division consisted of three infantry brigades commanded by Brigadier General Willis A. Gorman, Brigadier General Frederick W. Lander and Colonel Edward D. Baker. While Baker served as a brigade commander, his own California Regiment was commanded by his friend, Lieutenant Colonel Isaac Wistar. There were two New York regiments in Stone's division. One of them, the 42nd New York, was known as the Tammany Regiment and was commanded by Colonel Milton Cogswell.

Colonel Cogswell was a good soldier and a handsome one, standing six feet, one inch tall, with fine features and a heavy beard. His only child, Susan, had been born on August 13, only a few days before he left New York with his regiment; it was to be many months before he saw his wife and baby daughter again. Cogswell was a regular army officer and an 1849 West Point graduate ranking 11th (in a class of 42). He was an infantry captain when the war began, and he might have remained a captain had it not been for the influence of his father-in-law, William Jared Lane, a justice of the New York Supreme Court. Unlike the Confederacy, the Union kept its regular army officers with regular units; as a result, only 248 of the 1,080 regular army officers on duty when the war began ever reached the rank of colonel or higher. Thanks to Judge Lane's political influence, Cogswell was rocketed to the rank of colonel and the command of Tammany Hall's own regiment. (It was carried as an "independent organization," neither a militia nor a volunteer unit.)

When Cogswell was elected to the Order of Tammany in early August, he promised to take care that the Tammany Regiment should not lose its good name and that "no inefficient officers led the men into the field," but he had no control over the efficiency of his own superiors, and this was to be a matter for regret.

Also included in Stone's division were two and a half batteries of artillery—the 6th New York Independent Battery; Battery B, 1st Rhode Island Artillery; and a section (two guns) of Battery I, 1st United States Artillery—as well as six companies of the 3rd New York Cavalry, known as Van Alen's Cavalry.

In the early days on the shores of the Potomac pickets exchanged shots across the river, but few, if any, were actually killed in these long range exchanges of fire. Lieutenant Richard Derby of the 15th Massachusetts wrote home about a man who was wounded in the arm while washing dishes in the river, but most of the shots fired were scarcely more dangerous than the taunts and jeers that were frequently thrown back and forth.

After awhile curiosity overcame belligerence and in places the opposing pickets became quite friendly. At Edwards Ferry the 1st Minnesota pickets put up a swing. Corporal Sam Stebbins wrote home: "I have often seen them sit and swing for a long time right in sight of the enemy." A soldier in the 15th Massachusetts made a truce with a Mississippi soldier, and they waded out to meet each other at a shallow spot on the river where the water was only waist high. They exchanged newspapers—the Boston *Herald* for the Mobile *Tribune*—and had a chat. Both agreed that "the shooting of pickets is all foolishness."

For troops stationed along the Potomac, the fall of 1861 was marked by inactivity and boredom. Pickets kept an eye on the opposing shore and reconnaissances were made, but friendly exchanges also took place. Such meetings eventually became commonplace; but after Ball's Bluff, still in the first year of the war, the meetings involving Stone's command were used to cast doubt on his loyalty.

Union pickets guarding the Potomac's Maryland shore.

The pickets finally became so neighborly that occasionally they would cross the river and pay visits. Stone tried to put a stop to this. He issued orders to his own troops and sent Captain Clinton Berry over the river under a flag of truce to tell the Confederates that intercourse between the pickets must cease and that if he caught one of the Confederates on the Maryland side, he would have him arrested and shot. The Confederate officer to whom Berry gave the message readily agreed to do the same.

Many of the men enjoyed picket duty, for it freed them

A reconnaissance along the banks of the Potomac.

Meeting of Union and Confederate pickets in a river. Note figure lounging on the far bank.

56

Pickets trading between the lines.

from drill and camp fatigues. The Union pickets, strung out along the towpath of the Chesapeake and Ohio Canal that parallels the river, remained on duty for several days at a time. They had no tents, but they made little huts for themselves and tried to thatch them with weeds. One soldier wrote that they were "living like Indians." Their worst annoyance was the swarms of insects that descended upon them.

It was in many ways a pleasant time. The weather was good, the surroundings beautiful, the food gradually improved, and many found life on the upper Potomac healthy and delightful, although there were those who were "bitterly afflicted" by homesickness. Letters from home helped. Mail came in three times a week, and often the regimental chaplain acted as postmaster. While some men wrote letters to go out with every mail, one man in the 15th Massachusetts served for three years and never wrote a line.

Chaplains were kept busy. British-born William G. Scandlin, thirty-three, was chaplain of the 15th Massachusetts.
He had served ten years in the Royal Navy and spent three
years on whalers before becoming a Unitarian minister. He
was a "great, hearty, whole-souled man, intensely in earnest
in whatever he undertook." Scandlin not only acted as regimental postmaster, but also as librarian, forming a regimental
library of several hundred volumes. On Sundays he preached
from a pulpit formed by a drum supported by a stack of muskets;
on his right hand was the regimental flag made by the ladies
of Worcester, and on his left the state flag of Massachusetts.

The 15th Massachusetts appears to have been an exceptionally religious regiment. In addition to the regular Sunday
service, it held prayer meetings in the evening, and on
Wednesdays too. Private Ai Osborne in a letter home spoke
disapprovingly of the profanity he heard in the army, and
added piously, "When I return, as I trust I shall, I hope no
one will ever have occasion to blush with shame for any habits
or vices which I have contracted in the U.S. service." Lieutenant W.J. Coulter told those at home:

> Sunday is kept by the soldiers of the Fifteenth al-
> most as strictly as it would be if it were at
> home. . . . On Sunday evening . . . everything is
> tranquil, and from many of the quarters songs of
> praise to God float out upon the air. It puts one in
> mind of a camp meeting more than it does of a mil-
> itary encampment. . . . In some of the tents the
> boys make it a practice of reading every night from
> the Testaments presented to them.

On weekday evenings there were other diversions. Each
regiment had its band and choruses were formed. In the 15th
Massachusetts Private Charlie May would bring out his fiddle;
"an old barn door would serve as a floor for dancing, and a
jolly evening would be spent." Nearby Poolesville held en-

ticements. An entrepreneur had set up a "daguerrotype shop on wheels", and a soldier could dress up and have his picture taken for the folks back home. There were strict orders against gambling and drinking, but there were always several whiskey peddlers in the town and around the camps. The abstinence of the men of Company H, 11th Massachusetts, who took the pledge to be teetotal for the duration of their service because "their business is to fight, not drink," was an exception to the prevailing spirit in the army."

The 20th Massachusetts had trouble with liquor even before it left home. The regiment was formed in July and set up camp about eight miles outside Boston at Readsville Station. The regimental historian noted that "it was a long time before the men could appreciate that they must remain in camp, even when off duty, and must not follow their own sweet will in going up to Klemm's at Mill Village for a sociable glass of beer." A considerable number drank more than beer, and the resulting drunkenness caused Major Paul Revere to lead the adjutant and a detail of men in a raid on Klemm's, where he confiscated the liquor and had it dumped in the street. Challenged for his authority to do this, he laid his pistol on the bar with the words, "This is my authority."

The editor of the Worcester *Spy*, after visiting the camp of the 15th Massachusetts in Maryland reported that "there are enough here who would sell whiskey if they dared, but Colonel Devens is a mortal terror to all such fellows." The Colonel of the 1st Minnesota was perhaps not such a terror to whiskey peddlers for, in spite of his ferocious-sounding name—Colonel Napoleon Jackson Tecumseh Dana—they sold whiskey to his men. When two slaves belonging to a Maryland planter were caught selling liquor to some 1st Minnesota boys, Brigadier General Willis Gorman, the brigade commander, took charge of the matter and sent for their master to ask what should be done with the culprits. The planter protested that "he didn't like to meddle in military matters" but suggested that their last customers should be made to give the "black rascals" a sound whipping. Gorman arranged it.

Minnesota soldiers could be made to whip slaves, but it is doubtful that such an order could have been executed in some regiments without provoking a mutiny. Runaway Virginia slaves sometimes slipped across the river and were sheltered in the lines of Massachusetts regiments; slaves belonging to Maryland planters were also welcomed among the abolitionist Massachusetts men until General Stone put a stop to it.

There were as yet no black units in the Union army, although the idea of forming them had been discussed. Governor Andrew was eager to organize regiments of black infantry, but Governor David Tod of Ohio thought that "to enlist Negro soldiers would be to drive every white man out of the service," and Lincoln was also against such units for political reasons, saying that arming blacks "would turn 50,000 bayonets from the loyal border states against us." Not for another year would a black regiment see battle, and it was not until March 2, 1863, that Frederick Douglass issued his stirring appeal: "Men of color, to arms!" But at least one free black, Lewis A. Bell of Washington, D.C., who was serving as Colonel Cogswell's orderly, took part in the battle that broke the peaceful routine of life on the upper Potomac. Although no history has recorded his actions and fame has eluded him, Bell was probably the first black to fight in the Civil War.

4.
A Slight Demonstration

Sickness plagued the 8th Virginia and the regiment was reduced to about 400 effectives when it marched into Loudoun County. Its colonel, Eppa Hunton, suffering from a fistula, was being cared for at the home of his mother in neighboring Fauquier County. There on October 17th or 18th he had a premonition; "I became satisfied that there was a movement on foot in the army and a fight pending." If there was to be a battle, he wanted to be in it. So, over the objections of his relatives and friends, he had his bed put in a wagon and set off to rejoin his regiment. On the night of October 19 he found his men camped in a field belonging to Dr. T. Claggett a few miles south of Leesburg. His "brave boys" were glad to see him, for many thought that the second-in-command, Lieutenant Colonel Charles Tebbs, was "too excitable for a safe commander."

The next day, October 20, 1861, was a Sunday. Across the river in Maryland 20-year-old First Lieutenant Oliver Wendell Holmes, Jr., sat in the doorway of his tent and watched a black hawk wheel slowly over the river some two miles downstream. It was a beautiful warm autumn day, and the maple trees along the river flamed yellow. Lieutenant Colonel Francis Palfrey had read the church service that morning, and young Holmes had thoughts of his parents, how at the same time back in Boston they too were attending church services.

His thoughts and the stillness of the early afternoon were broken at two o'clock by the sharp tap of a drum beating "assembly."

The soldiers did not yet know, but this was their call to arms, announcing that the time had come to put an end to fatigues and drill and listless gazing at the river. It was time now to do that which they had been brought from their homes to do here on the shores of the Potomac, time now to validate their manhood, time to suffer the bitter realities of war. It was to be many months before young Holmes would again lounge in his tent's doorway or would again know the peace he felt that morning. He would never again be that same boy.

Although General Stone had put in motion Holmes's regiment and several others, he did not intend that they should do any fighting just yet—but not much that happened in the next forty-eight hours was as Stone intended. What worried Stone in Poolesville and McClellan in Washington was what the enemy intended to do. Was Evans going to be reinforced and then attack across the river, or was he going to retreat up Goose Creek to the Confederate's main positions around Centreville?

Two months earlier, on August 18, when Stone had scarcely arrived at Poolesville, McClellan had sent him a message: "Information from General Banks to-day confirms that the enemy intends crossing the Potomac in your vicinity and moving on Baltimore or Washington." Stone, however, had disagreed, and the next day he had told McClellan that he believed there were only two Mississippi regiments in the neighborhood of Leesburg, and he noted that "the constant rains for the past week must have made the roads very bad on the low grounds on the opposite side of the river and have made the fords at least a foot deeper." He added that if McClellan still thought the Confederates could cross, he ought to send him two more regiments of infantry.

McClellan supplied more troops and continued to believe, as he told Secretary of War Cameron on September 6, that although he expected the enemy to make demonstrations elsewhere, the "main and real movement will be to cross the Potomac between Washington and Point of Rocks. . . . His hope will be . . . to move with a large force direct and unopposed on Baltimore." Such an estimate was based upon fears, not facts. McClellan's forces were nearly double those of Confederate General Joseph Johnston opposite him in northern Virginia, but he did not know this and he feared a Confederate attack before he had built up his army and trained it. He was anxious to avoid a premature action, he told Cameron, for "the fate of the nation and the success of the cause in which we are engaged must be mainly decided by the issue of the next battle to be fought by the army under my command." But when that battle came, McClellan was completely unprepared for it and the battle decided nothing.

Although the Confederates had made no attempt to cross the Potomac, Evans's brigade near Leesburg continued to worry McClellan and Stone, for they lacked a clear idea of the size and disposition of the Confederate force on the Virginia shore. Spies had been sent across the river, but spying was an inexact science. Stone and Evans each knew the other was there but, surprising in view of the ease with which civilians still crossed the Potomac, neither knew the strength of the other and, because adequate military maps were nonexistent, the nature of the terrain on the opposite shore was almost as unknown as the African interior. Evans's total force consisted of fewer than 2,000 men, but Francis Buxton, a Union spy, had reported to McClellan's headquarters on October 6 that "the forces at Leesburg have been kept up to nearly 27,000." However, two days later the New York *Daily Tribune*, without disclosing its sources, if any, confidently told its readers: "There is hardly a doubt that we shall presently hear of a retreat inland by the rebels opposite General Stone."

On October 13 Stone had telegraphed McClellan that he "anticipated an early attempt by the enemy to secure Mason's or Harrison's Island, perhaps both, but probably the latter." Five days later, however, he reported that the Confederate pickets had been withdrawn from most of the posts in front of him. The following day he sent a situation report, passing on some information given him by "an intelligent mulatto teamster, who deserted from the Thirteenth Mississippi Regiment, near Leesburg" to the effect that the Confederates under Evans, alarmed by the prospect of a Federal force crossing the Potomac, were prepared for flight. Stone said he believed this to be true and added that he had "prepared slight entrenchments on Harrison's Island."

Although McClellan wanted to avoid any precipitate action, he was beginning to feel the political pressure to do something with his army. The phrase repeated so often in the newspapers, "all quiet along the Potomac," was already becoming a joke and a rebuke for his inaction. If indeed the Confederates felt nervous about their exposed troops at Leesburg and they could be induced to flee by a slight effort on his part, it would seem worth a try; perhaps something might then be gained with little risk. In any case, a movement forward in Virginia would give him a chance to learn more about its topography. So McClellan decided to push McCall's division, already opposite Washington in Virginia, up the Potomac towards Dranesville, about twelve miles southeast of Leesburg, to study the lay of the land and to see if the Confederates would take fright. On October 20 he sent a message to Stone through his assistant adjutant general:

> Gen. McClellan desires me to inform you that General McCall occupied Drainesville [sic] yesterday, and is still there. He will send out heavy reconnaissances today in all directions from that point. The General desires that you keep a good

lookout upon Leesburg to see if this movement has the effect to drive them away. Perhaps a slight demonstration on your part would have the effect to move them.

Evans, meanwhile, having captured a courier of McCall's, learned before Stone did of McCall's move on Dranesville and had the previous night moved the bulk of his brigade to Burnt Bridge (a spot where the Leesburg turnpike crossed Goose Creek) and had taken up a position on the northwest bank. He had not, however, withdrawn all his pickets along the Potomac.

At one o'clock in the afternoon on October 20 Stone went down to Edwards Ferry with Gorman's brigade plus the 7th Michigan, two troops of cavalry and some artillery. He threw a few shells across the river, but they did no damage. Evans kept an eye on his activity but was not unduly disturbed by the cannonade. Stone ordered troops down to the river at Edwards Ferry and opposite Harrison's Island; he even sent a small force across the river at Edwards Ferry, then quickly brought them back again. Such was the "slight demonstration" McClellan had asked him to make. But Evans was no more deceived than he had been by McDowell's feint towards the stone bridge at Bull Run. He was close enough to Edwards Ferry to shift his forces there if he had to; it was only two miles away. He was also in a position to retreat up Goose Creek to Centreville if need be, but he was not to be frightened off by Stone's maneuverings.

Although the demonstration appeared to have little effect upon Evans, Stone could not be sure. He was not even certain the Confederates were still there. Perhaps they had abandoned Leesburg. Earlier, on October 4, Captain Chase Philbrick of the 15th Massachusetts had scouted Harrison's Island. As he had found only an ancient slave called "Old Phil" and some dilapidated buildings there, Stone ordered the island occupied and entrenchments made. Now, as no pickets had been seen on the opposite shore for two days, he sent an order to Colonel Devens to send Captain Philbrick back with a reconnaissance party on a more dangerous mission across to the Virginia shore. Stone sent his order about noon, but Devens had "gone to church or something of that sort," as Stone later explained, and it was not until several hours later that he received the order, and it was not until sunset that Philbrick, taking Lieutenant Church Howe and twenty men, set forth. By this time, Stone, thinking the reconnaissance must have been completed, was impatiently waiting for his report. This delay, resulting in the reconnaissance being carried out at night rather than in daylight, was the first of a series of mistakes and misfortunes that was to mark a path to disaster.

Only a few months earlier, Philbrick, age thirty-eight, had been a stonecutter in Northbridge, Massachusetts now he commanded Company H of the 15th Massachusetts. Howe, twenty-three, was an accountant who had enlisted as a private but whose business acumen had enabled him to rise from the ranks, and he was now the regimental quartermaster of the Fifteenth. Philbrick's orders, according to Stone, were "to cross from the island and explore by a path through the woods, little used, in the direction of Leesburg, to see if he could find anything concerning the enemy's position in that direction."

It took several hours for Philbrick and his party to cross over to Harrison's Island, traverse it, row to the Virginia shore, and then climb Ball's Bluff and head towards Leesburg. By this time it was a fine moonlight night with some autumn haze. They were able to go to within about two miles (Philbrick said one mile) of the town without encountering any signs of the enemy. Then Philbrick saw what he took to be about thirty tents. He approached to within 130 yards, according to his own account, but he saw neither camp fires nor sentinels. With this information, he scurried back, reaching the safety of Harrison's Island about ten o'clock.

Historians have recorded that the battle of Ball's Bluff was triggered by McClellan's order for a "slight demonstration," but this is inaccurate, for Stone had already completed his demonstration without the loss of a man. What followed next, as Stone readily admitted later to a congressional committee, was the result of his own initiative based on his original orders from McClellan, given him on August 11, the day before he assumed command of his Corps of Observation:

> *You will keep the main body of your force united in a strong position near Poolesville, and observe the dangerous fords with strong pickets that can dispute the passage until re-enforced. . . . Should you see the opportunity of capturing or dispersing any small parties by crossing the river, you are at liberty to do so, though great discretion is recommended in making such a movement. The general object of your command is to observe and dispute the passage of the river and the advance of the enemy. . . I leave your operations much to your own discretion, in which I have the fullest confidence.*

Stone's orders were clear: he could make little raids if he saw the chance and was careful, but he was not to provoke a battle.

The intelligence brought back by Captain Philbrick pleased Stone; he thought he saw "a very nice little military chance." It did not seem peculiar or cause him to question the accuracy of the report that Philbrick and Howe had seen neither camp fires nor sentinels. "It seemed to me," he said later, "precisely one of those pieces of carelessness on the part of the enemy that ought to be taken advantage of." He therefore decided on a small raid and ordered Colonel Devens to take four companies (Devens understood five companies, about 300 men) across the river at Ball's Bluff and destroy the camp.

His return was to be covered by Colonel Lee and a hundred

men of the 20th Massachusetts who would wait for him at the top of the bluff. Stone's orders were not entirely clear. "Colonel Devens," he said later, "was ordered to use this opportunity to observe the approaches to Leesburg and the position and force of any enemy in the vicinity, and in case he found no enemy or found him only weak, and a position where he could observe well and be secure until his party could be strengthened sufficiently to make a valuable reconnaissance which should safely ascertain the position and force of the enemy, to hold on and report."

There were a number of "ifs" in this order and much depended upon Devens's assessment of the situation after he had destroyed the Confederate camp and on his judgment as to what he ought to do. Nevertheless, Devens started out about midnight with five companies of his regiment and at once encountered difficulties. The Potomac was swollen and the current was swift. To carry his force across from Harrison's Island to the Virginia shore there were only three boats with a total capacity of twenty-five to thirty men. It was four o'clock in the morning before he got his men over, but at last they were all on the Virginia side undetected, and they started up a "narrow sheep path" to the top of Ball's Bluff. Colonel Lee then followed with 101 men from companies E and I of the 20th Massachusetts.

The side of the bluff was covered with trees and bushes, but on top lay an irregularly shaped open field of about six to eight acres covered with "wild grass, scrub oak and locust trees." A small road ran through the field and curved to the left into the woods beyond. Captain Philbrick led the way down the road for about a mile until they reached a heavy rail fence on the further side of the woods. Beyond was another field of about the same size as the first; this extended to the right as far as the road that ran from Leesburg to Conrad's Ferry. When Devens and his men reached the point where Philbrick had seen the Confederate camp, they saw at the end of the field in front of them a slight ridge with a single row of trees on top. There was no Confederate camp, no row of tents, only the line of trees. In an uncertain light, viewed by a nervous observer, the spaces between them might have resembled tents. Philbrick had not, as he certainly ought to have done, moved close enough to be sure of what he was seeing. Of such small mistakes are tragedies contrived.

As soon as Philbrick's mistake was discovered, Devens sent Lieutenant Church Howe back to General Stone (who made his headquarters near Edwards Ferry this day) to report that the Confederate camp did not exist and that there was no sign of the enemy.

Meanwhile, to divert Confederate attention from Devens and to make a reconnaissance of the area between Edwards Ferry and Leesburg, Stone had ordered General Gorman to throw across the river at Edwards Ferry two companies of the 1st Minnesota and thirty-one cavalry under cover of a battery on the Maryland shore. Once across, the infantry was ordered to deploy as skirmishers around the bridgehead while the cavalry, under Major John Mix, was "to advance along the Leesburg road until they should come to the vicinity of a battery which was known to be on that road and then turn to the left, and examine the heights between that and Goose Creek, to see if any of the enemy were posted in the vicinity, ascertain as nearly as possible their number and disposition, examine the country with reference to the passage of troops to the Leesburg and Georgetown turnpike, and return rapidly to cover behind the skirmishers of the Minnesota First."

All went very much as planned with Major Mix and his reconnaissance. He encountered some of the Mississippi volunteers and his troop received their fire at thirty-five yards, but they returned it with their pistols; the only loss was one horse. Major Mix galloped back with a prisoner. Stone, reporting the action to McClellan, called it "a gallant reconnaissance."

The day must have seemed bright and promising to General Stone that morning. On receiving Lieutenant Howe's report that Devens had advanced within sight of Leesburg without seeing any sign of the enemy, he began to think that his troops might be able to maintain a position in Virginia near Ball's Bluff at least long enough to reconnoiter the area. He decided to put Colonel Edward Baker in charge of the operation and he sent for him. Before Baker arrived, Stone gave orders for ten cavalrymen to be sent to Devens so that he could scout the countryside, and for howitzers to be stationed on the towpath of the C&O Canal on the Maryland side. He also sent orders to Lieutenant Colonel George H. Ward* to lead the remaining five companies of the 15th Massachusetts across the river and to take up a position at Smart's Mill, a solid stone building located on the Virginia side a half mile north of Ball's Bluff. This was a shrewd concept. The mill was on low ground with open fields around it that could be covered by guns from Harrison's Island. It was a position that could be easily held if the Union forces on the Virginia shore should be driven back. There were no bluffs and it was easier to cross the river here. Had Stone's orders been obeyed, the outcome of the battle of Ball's Bluff would certainly have been quite different.

We have only Stone's version of what took place during his meeting with Baker at Edwards Ferry that morning, but there is no reason to believe that what was said was substantially different from what he reported; his written orders given to Baker tend to confirm his story. It was a fateful meeting.

Stone was at this time a brigadier general doing a major general's job; Baker was a colonel with a brigadier general's command. Stone was a West Pointer with a military education and years of professional experience, including distinguished

---

*Ward, 35 years old and second in command of the 15th Massachusetts, was a descendant of General Artemus Ward of Revolutionary War fame.

war service; Baker's military experience was limited to a few months service during the Mexican War. Given this much, the superior-subordinate relationship would appear normal and comfortable for both men. But there were other factors which suggest that this was not the case, that the chain of command was not as clear cut as it ought to have been, and that Stone's relations with this particular subordinate might not have been entirely comfortable for him.

Ten months earlier, Stone had been merely a former junior officer who had left the service to become a not-so-successful businessman; he was an unknown, and only thirty-seven years old. Baker, fifty, was a United States senator, a close friend of president Lincoln, and a nationally known public figure. In the Mexican War Baker had been a colonel; Stone had been a lieutenant. In this war, Baker had already been offered a brigadier's star, but had refused the promotion in order to preserve his seat in the Senate.* Exactly one month earlier, on September 21, he had been appointed a major general, but he had not yet decided whether to accept or refuse the appointment. Thus, he could at any moment he chose accept the promotion and instantly become Stone's superior. All this Stone must have known. Although some officers in Stone's division complained of the imperious manner in which he gave orders, it is doubtful that he took a high tone with Edward Baker; this was a subordinate to be treated with kid gloves. He obviously felt it was safe to entrust Baker with discretionary powers—the same discretionary powers he himself had been given by McClellan—and he gave Baker the same cautionary advice that McClellan had given him.

In his report, written eight days later, Stone said that he

---

*On August 2 the Senate had confirmed the appointment to the rank of brigadier general of both Stone and Baker; also appointed at the same time were Sherman, Porter, Hooker, Lander and three others. Four days later, in his last speech in the Senate, Baker declined the appointment.

had had "a full conversation" with Baker and that he had told him of McCall's advance on Dranesville; "detailed to him the means of transportation across the river, of the sufficiency of which he was to be the judge;" told him of his intention to pass more troops across the river at Edwards Ferry, and cautioned him that there were breastworks and a "hidden battery" between Ball's Bluff and Edwards Ferry, which would prevent any movement north. He then "left it to Baker's discretion, after viewing the ground, to retire the troops from the Virginia shore under cover of his guns and the fire of the large infantry force, or to pass over re-enforcements in case he found it practicable and the position on the other side strong and favorable." He went on to explain that he was "extremely desirous of ascertaining the exact position and force of the enemy in our front" and of exploring "as far as it was safe" the area around Leesburg, but emphasized that he "wished no advance unless the enemy were in inferior force." He assigned to Baker, in addition to Baker's own brigade, the 42nd New York (Tammany Regiment) and the 15th and 20th Massachusetts. Later Stone told the Joint Committee on the Conduct of the War:

> I had carefully instructed him in the morning that
> he was not to fight a superior force there; that if in
> his observation of Colonel Devens the advance
> should come upon a strong force, he was to retire
> suddenly into entrenchments that I had prepared on
> Harrison's Island, this advance [sic] being covered
> by the artillery on this side, and the troops of
> Baker's brigade.

Stone's orders to Baker, like McClellan's to him, reflected a hope that a slight push would cause the Confederates to fall back, to retreat up Goose Creek. If they did not yield to this pressure, Stone had no intention of forcing the issue. He was a soldier who obeyed orders; his instructions allowed him to make a slight push; he had no authority to shove, and he had no intention of doing so.

The difference between a push and a shove is a matter of degree, of course, and so is subject to misunderstanding. McClellan and Stone were of one mind; both of these professional soldiers understood the delicate difference. Stone undoubtedly tried to explain the difference to Baker, and he undoubtedly thought Baker understood. He had every reason to believe that Baker, a mature man accustomed to responsibility and capable of perceiving the national interest, would not act irresponsibly. He could not know that Baker possessed a streak of rashness which, combined with his martial romanticism, would prove fatal for him and for his enterprise.

Baker was not a man whose thoughts focused on subtle differences. For him the world was filled with the good and the bad, the right and the wrong, the just and the unjust; there were no grey areas. He used qualifying adjectives to magnify rather than refine nouns. Thus, he could say without blinking—as he once did—that the United States possessed "a perfect system of morality." He was not the sort of man who could easily comprehend the difference between a light push and a shove. Nor was he a man who did things by halves. He threw himself wholeheartedly and in the grand manner into whatever he did. He was a plunger: at the faro tables, in politics, in life. He was, in short, a man who by intellect and by instinct preferred the battle to the skirmish.

There are times, of course, when "Damn the torpedoes! Full speed ahead!" is both the bravest and the wisest course. But not always. It is usually best if such determinations follow an appraisal of the situation and a thoughtful consideration of alternatives. But Baker was not a thinker; he talked too much to have time to think. In his political career a remarkable memory served in lieu of a keen intellect. What Stone asked him to do—make an assessment of the situation and decide whether to fight or withdraw—was not only beyond his capability but alien to his nature. Baker was the wrong man to take command at Ball's Bluff that day.

Baker asked for his orders in writing so that he "would have some written authority for assuming command," and Stone hastily scribbled a summary:

> *Colonel: In case of heavy firing in front of Harrison's Island, you will advance the California regiment of your brigade or retire the regiments under Colonels Lee and Devens upon the Virginia side of the river, at your discretion, assuming command on arrival.*

Just as, when he was a lawyer, Baker had carried in his hat such few notes and papers as he thought he needed, so now he stuck Stone's order in his hat. In the evening it was found there, stained with his blood. Later it was to be carefully scrutinized, interpreted and misinterpreted.

It would appear that Baker wanted his orders in writing not only as proof that he had a right to assume command, but also to show that he had discretionary power. Whether Baker did not understand Stone's orders or whether he chose deliberately to ignore them, we will never know, but the best evidence indicates that from the moment he left Stone at Edwards Ferry at about 9:30 that morning and galloped down the towpath to take up his command, Baker was intent on pushing as many troops as possible across the river and doing battle with any Confederates he found there. If the light push did not succeed, Baker was ready, eager even, to shove, and to shove hard.

5.
The Battle Begins
✳ ✳ ✳

For the past two months Captain W.L. Duff, commanding Company K of the 17th Mississippi, had been detailed to watch Ball's Bluff and the Union troops over on Harrison's Island. He was camped with his company two miles northeast of Leesburg at a place called Big Spring, part of a thousand-acre farm owned by George Washington Ball, a nephew of the first president and the man who gave his name to the bluffs that overlooked the river.

One of Duff's pickets discovered Lee's men, or rather, Lee's men found the picket. Colonel Lee, after distributing his two companies along the top of the bluff, had sent out scouting parties from both flanks. On the right, Adjutant Charles Peirson with a sergeant and three men from Company I peered incautiously into a gully and stumbled upon Duff's picket. Shots were exchanged and 29-year-old First Sergeant William Riddle of Boston was hit by a bullet in his right elbow, becoming the first casualty of the battle.

As soon as the picket reported the news of the Federal crossing to Captain Duff, Lieutenant Joseph Harten was sent pounding off to Evans, still on Goose Creek. Meanwhile, Duff hastily gathered up all the men he could lay hands on, about forty, and set off to do battle. His report of the first sight of the invaders (Devens's men) has the homely touch of a man moving in a familiar landscape: "When we reached the top of the hill near Mrs. Steven's house we saw the skirmishers of the enemy on the left, and in large force in Mrs. Jackson's

75

yard in front." Size is relative, of course, and to Captain Duff, with only forty men and the nearest help two miles away, Devens's 300 men looked like a "large force." But Duff's actions were heroic: he put his men behind fences and opened fire.

Lieutenant Harten reached Evans about six o'clock that morning. At about the same time, Evans received word that the Union troops had also crossed at Edwards Ferry. He could now see danger in three directions: the possible movement of McCall's force down the Leesburg Pike from Dranesville; the Union crossing at Edwards Ferry; and the crossing at Ball's Bluff. He must have felt exposed and vulnerable, as indeed he was. It would have been a simple operation, and excusable, had he pulled in his men and backed off, retreating south along Goose Creek, but he neither retreated nor called for reinforcements. For the time being, he waited and watched.

Evans appears to have been, at first, more concerned about the crossing at Edwards Ferry than the crossing at Ball's Bluff, but he shifted his headquarters to Fort Evans so as to be able to keep an eye on both places. It was not until nine o'clock— three hours after learning of the Ball's Bluff crossing—that he decided he could afford to send reinforcements to Duff: Lieutenant Colonel Jenifer with two companies of the 18th Mississippi plus some seventy of his own cavalry.

It was nearly seven o'clock in the morning when Duff's men opened fire on the Federals; Devens immediately sent forward Captain Philbrick's Company H to drive them off. Duff retreated about 300 yards down the hill towards Leesburg, then he halted his company in the open and turned to face the line of Union troops as they steadily advanced toward him, their arms held at the "make ready." Duff then did a curious thing; he called out to the advancing troops to halt. He did this five or six times. The response of Philbrick's soldiers was equally curious; each time Duff cried "Halt!" they replied "Friends!" Philbrick and his men advanced to within sixty yards of the Confederates, neither side firing a shot, before Duff awoke to the reality that the war was not to be halted and that these young men from Massachusetts were not the friends of his young men from Mississippi. They had all traveled a long way from their homes to meet in bitter combat on this pleasant Loudoun field. Duff gave the order to kneel and fire.

The volley broke the Union line and stopped it; a second volley caused Philbrick's men to fall back. Reinforced, they returned to the fight. For twenty minutes the Mississippi and Massachusetts men exchanged fire, then Devens ordered his troops back to the heavy rail fence on the edge of the woods just south of Mrs. Jackson's house, and they fell back in good order, carrying with them most of their dead and wounded. Devens had lost one man killed, two missing and nine wounded; Duff had one man seriously wounded and two slightly wounded.

Duff also drew back, for he feared the Union troops might try to get behind him and cut the road between Big Spring and Leesburg. He had moved back about three hundred yards and was on the road himself when he discovered that Jenifer's force had arrived and some of the 18th Mississippi were in earthworks on his right flank. Thus encouraged, he moved forward again.

Devens does not appear to have been greatly concerned at this time, although when Lieutenant Howe returned, he sent him back immediately to tell General Stone of the skirmish and to report that he was still under attack. On his way back, Howe encountered Colonel Lee on the top of the bluff; Lee was in fine spirits and gave Howe another message to deliver: "Tell Stone," he said, "that if he wants to open a campaign in Virginia, now is the time."

Howe crossed over to Harrison's Island and there met Lieutenant Colonel Ward, who was engaged in the slow process of passing over the river to the island in the few available boats the remaining half of the 15th Massachusetts. While Howe waited for a boat to take him to the Maryland shore, the two men discussed the situation. Devens was in a "tight place," Howe said, and needed his support. Convinced that Devens had actually asked for his help, Ward told Howe that Stone had ordered him to occupy Smart's Mill, but that as Devens needed him, he would go to his support. It was an unfortunate decision.

Perhaps Ward, like his men, was overly eager for action and preferred joining Devens to occupying Smart's Mill. Private George Simonds of Company B, a gentle, quiet young man of "almost boyish appearance," later described the feelings of Ward's men when they received orders to cross the river: "I think we never marched six or seven miles easier than we did that morning. We all knew and felt that 'something was up.' We all hoped that before the next morning something would be done." Simonds's brother, Captain Clark Simonds, a tall, 30-year-old scythe-maker, his company commander, was wounded before he reached the battlefield. He slipped on a rolling stone and in trying to regain his balance ran the point of his sword into the side of his head, cutting a great gash in his scalp. He was advised to go back but instead tied a white handkerchief around his head saying, "No, if there is to be a fight, I want to be with my men." *

Charles H. Eager, thirty-one, who five months before had been a hardware dealer in Fitchburg, Massachusetts, and was now a lieutenant in Captain Simonds's company, later told his wife: "I felt, and I presume all others did, as though it might be each individual self that would be spared. As we were crossing the river I looked the men over and wondered *who it would be.* I felt then *all* of us *could not* return and that some of us were leaving the *Union line* for the last time."

---

*Captain Simonds survived the battle of Ball's Bluff, but his two younger brothers were wounded. All three Simonds brothers were killed in the war. Clark Simonds, killed at Antietam, left a wife and two children.

When Lieutenant Howe had crossed over from Harrison's Island to the Maryland shore and started down the towpath to Edwards Ferry, he encountered Colonel Baker, and described to him, as far as he understood it, the situation on Ball's Bluff. "I am going down immediately with my whole force and take command," Baker said, and, spurring his horse, galloped off.

At Edwards Ferry Howe reported to Stone; he told him of the skirmish, gave him Colonel Lee's message, and told him that Ward, instead of occupying Smart's Mill, was going to reinforce Devens. "Colonel Baker is at that place and will arrange these things to suit himself," Stone said calmly. He added only a few words of warning, instructing Howe to caution Baker to be careful of his right flank. To McClellan he telegraphed: "The enemy has been engaged opposite Harrison's Island. Our men are behaving admirably."

On his way back to Ball's Bluff, Howe, finding Baker by the river bank, still on the Maryland shore, asked if he had any orders for Devens regarding his dispositions, but Baker replied that Devens and his men "had done nobly." He could take up any position he liked.

Howe thought it was about eleven o'clock by the time he made his way back to Devens, but probably it was at least an hour later. During his absence Devens had again been attacked. Jenifer's force, swollen to about 320 men by the addition of Duff's company, had at eleven o'clock (according to Jenifer) or noon (according to Devens) launched an attack on the left of Devens's line. The Federals held their ground, however, and Jenifer's men fell back and took cover behind a high fence, keeping up a hot fire. Devens too drew back uncertainly, at first only about sixty paces, where he put his men in an open space in a wood. Then, in the face of continuing Confederate fire, he retreated to Lee's position at the top of the bluff. However, finding that he was not pursued, he moved his line forward again, and his men took up good positions behind the heavy rail fence.

It was at this time that Howe reported back from Stone with the information that some cavalry was being sent over and that Baker was on his way to take command of the field. Devens by his movements back and forth appears to have been unsure of the enemy's strength and was perhaps debating whether or not he should retreat across the river. At this point, he probably could have done so with slight loss. However, the news Howe brought him of the appointment of Baker, whose only instruction was that Devens could take up any position he thought proper, seemed to indicate that he was expected to hold on and that he no longer had the discretionary authority to order a retreat. But if he was expected to stay and fight, he needed reinforcements, further orders, and some clarification of his mission. What now was the purpose of the troops on Ball's Bluff?

Devens dispatched Howe back to the river to look for Baker. Three times he did this. Infantry were crossing over, but Baker did not appear. Neither did the promised cavalry. The ten cavalrymen Stone had ordered for Devens did cross over to the Virginia side, and the officer in charge, Lieutenant Charles Candy, a regular army enlisted man who had recently been given a commission, climbed to the top of the bluff and reported to Lee, not to Devens. Although Lee seems to have given him no orders, Candy, for reasons never explained, simply turned around and took his cavalry back to Maryland. Devens said later: "If they had reported to me, they could have rendered excellent service."

Lieutenant Colonel Wistar with 570 men of the California Regiment was on the Maryland shore waiting for orders when the regimental chaplain, Robert Kellen, dashed up and said, "General Baker directs you, sir, to cross at once." Wistar immediately began the slow process of getting his men into the few boats and over to Harrison's Island. He had crossed six companies and had gone over himself when Baker, who had at last reached the island, rode up.

"Is that all the men you have got across?" he asked.

"Yes, sir."

"You must hurry all you can. Get everything that can float. Cross every man you can into Virginia. I'm going over now," Baker told him.

Ward's half of the 15th Massachusetts arrived on the field and reinforced Devens. Although Devens had not asked for the support, he was glad to get it, for Confederate bullets were taking their toll. Because no one had been appointed to look after the wounded, they were forced to care for themselves as best they could. Private George Simonds, hit in the thigh, saw his pants turn red and felt a shoe filling with blood. He started for the rear, making for some woods on the right of Devens's line. On the way he found two men from his regiment, Ai Osborn and Albert Litchfield, "sitting behind a corn stock," both had been shot. They were later captured. Simonds pushed on, "resolved to get back to friends or die." Coming upon a small house, he stopped for a moment to rest: "I found George Daniels, wounded in the wrist and shoulder. [Henry C.] Lowell, another of our boys, was there also. I saw him go to the corner and fire. 'There,' says he, 'I've fixed him. I saw him fall'."

On the Confederate side, Jenifer too was losing men. He sent a message back to Evans asking for reinforcements, but help was already on the way, for at ten o'clock Evans had concluded that the Union force crossing at Edwards Ferry was probably a feint and that the main attack was at Ball's Bluff. He therefore ordered Eppa Hunton and his "dear brave boys" of the 8th Virginia (less one company) to move to the support of Jenifer, telling him "to drive the enemy to the river" and that he would "support his right with artillery."

Both sides were now adding to their strength on the field, building the battle.

At 12:20 P.M. Eppa Hunton, still in pain but astride his horse and eager for battle, arrived on the field and, cooper-

Union troops shown advancing early in the battle.

ating with Jenifer's force, at once launched an attack on Devens's left.

Major Paul Revere with the remainder of the 20th Massachusetts reached Ball's Bluff between one and two o'clock in the afternoon. A private in the regiment said, "We marched up the hill, happy and gay, ready for the fight." On the path they met a soldier who called out, "You will have fun soon after you get to the top."

Colonel Lee, having received no orders from Baker, assumed that he was still to be the back-up force for Devens, so he placed his entire regiment in a line along the top of the bluff, facing west. Lieutenant Holmes's Company A was on the extreme left of the regiment's line. As soon as the 20th was across the river, two howitzers and a rifled James gun were sent over, and Lee positioned them in the open field by his own men.

There was a lull in the battle when the remainder of the 20th Massachusetts arrived. Some of the company officers gathered under a tree and sat smoking, listening to the officers from companies E and I describe their experiences that morning. When a shot was heard close by, old soldier Dreher said calmly in his German-accented voice, "Well, gentlemen, I advise you all to go to your companies."

In preparation for a hot fight, many of the men of the 20th Massachusetts had prudently taken off their grey coats with the scarlet linings and hung them on trees. When the first ragged Confederate volleys were fired, no one was hit, but the splendid overcoats were riddled with holes.

Baker, instead of crossing at once to Ball's Bluff and making an assessment of the situation, occupied himself on Harrison's Island in handling the first problem he encountered on the way: the bottleneck caused by the shortage of boats. Baker

83

had plenty of troops and he had ordered them forward at once, but they jammed up waiting to cross from Maryland's mainland to Harrison's Island and from the island to the foot of Ball's Bluff. For these two crossings there were never more than seven boats: two flatboats, two small ferry boats, two skiffs and one four-oared metallic lifeboat. Colonel Cogswell of the Tammany Regiment, who appears to have been the most intelligent senior officer on the field that day, later wrote:

> There were no guards at any of the landings. No boats' crews had been detailed, and each command as it arrived was obliged to organize its own. No guns were placed in position . . . to protect the passage . . . Had the full capacity of the boats been employed, more than twice as many men might have crossed in time to take part in the action.

Baker corrected none of these deficiencies, but he spent more than an hour personally supervising the lifting of a boat from the canal and its launching in the river—a task that ought to have been given to a junior officer—and in vainly trying to stretch a rope from the Maryland shore to Harrison's Island, a feat later performed by someone else. Meanwhile, the California Regiment under Lieutenant Colonel Wistar had crossed, and Cogswell's Tammany Regiment was struggling to get over. On the top of the bluff where the fighting was now heavy, no one was in overall command of the Union force.

Stone had received no reports from Baker. He assumed that all was well, but he felt the need to give some additional cautions and at 11:50 A.M. he sent Baker the following:

> COLONEL: I am informed that the force of the enemy is about 4,000, all told. If you push them, you may do so as far as to have a strong position near Leesburg, if you can keep them before you, avoid-

*ing their batteries. If they pass Leesburg and take
the Gum Spring road [towards Manassas] you will
not follow far, but seize the first good position to
cover that road. Their design is to draw us on, if
they are obliged to retreat, as far as Goose Creek,
where they can be re-enforced from Manassas and
have a strong position.*

*Report frequently, so that when they are pushed
Gorman can come in on their flank.*

Stone here revealed that he vastly overestimated Confederate strength, misjudged Evans's intentions, and had no intimation of the course which the battle would take. Baker was still on Harrison's Island when this message reached him about 1:30 P.M. The belief that his own force faced 4,000 Confederates did not daunt or deter him. He read the message, stuck it in his hat and replied:

*I acknowledge your order of 11:50, announcing
their force at 4,000. I have lifted a large boat out
of the canal into the river. I shall, as soon as I feel
strong enough, advance steadily, guarding my
flanks carefully. I will communicate with you
often. . . . As you know, I have ordered down my
brigade and Cogswell, who will cross as rapidly as
possible. I shall feel cautiously for them. I hope that
your movement below will give advantage. Please
communicate with me often.*

This message—the one and only message Stone ever received from Baker—is remarkable for what it implied and what it concealed. It did not reveal that Baker had not yet arrived on the field and that he had not even sent anyone to inquire what was happening on the Virginia shore. Though he must have heard the sounds of musketry, he made no mention of the fighting taking place; he did not speak of the confusion at the boats or of any other problem; and he did not display any hesitancy or doubts regarding his ability to deal with the Confederate force opposing him. His message breathed confidence and gave comforting assurances that care would be taken when he advanced, as he said he would. It gave no cause for alarm and not a hint of the problems involved in trying to move a large force across the river to push the Confederates out of Leesburg. Stone was certainly justified in inferring that Baker had made an assessment of the situation, that he saw no unsolvable problems, and that he would successfully carry out his orders while taking proper precautions.

At 2:00 P.M. Stone telegraphed McClellan:

> There has been sharp firing on the right of our line, and our troops appear to be advancing there under Baker. The left, under Gorman, has advanced its skirmishers nearly one mile, and, if the movement continues successfully, will turn the enemy's right.

Across the river, Evans watched the growing force at Edwards' Ferry and listened to reports from Ball's Bluff. Two or three times Major Norborne Berkeley had come to ask for more ammunition for the 8th Virginia. Later Hunton complained bitterly, "I got none at all and no excuse for the failure to send it." At 2:30 P.M. Hunton sent a volunteer aide, Elijah White, to Evans with a request for reinforcements, but Evans sent him back, saying, "Tell Hunton to fight on." Shortly thereafter Evans sent Colonel Burt and the 18th Mississippi to Ball's Bluff with orders to fall on the Federals' left flank.

At 3:30 P.M. Hunton again sent White back to ask for ammunition and reinforcements. Evans testily told him, "Tell Hunton to hold his ground till every damned man falls. *I have* sent him the Eighteenth and *will* send him the Seventeenth."

White galloped back to deliver this message, but on the way he encountered Lieutenant Colonel Tebbs leading part of the 8th Virginia off the field. They were already about 500 yards behind the firing line. White stopped and asked if Hunton had been whipped. Tebbs said he didn't know but that he had been ordered to fall back. White found Hunton, gave him Evans's message and asked if Tebbs had been ordered to retreat. "No," said Hunton with some heat. "Go and bring them right back to the line of battle." Tebbs turned back to the fight with most of the men—but not all. "Some of them went home," Hunton later admitted, "but not many."

Evans now decided to put all of his eggs into one basket, and he ordered Featherston's 17th Mississippi "to repair double-quick to the support of Colonel Burt." This was a bold gamble, for it left Evans with only nine companies of the 13th Mississippi, a reduced company of the 8th Virginia, and his six guns of the Richmond Howitzers to watch Gorman's brigade at Edwards Ferry.

Featherston moved with alacrity to get his regiment into action, and he reached the battlefield in twenty minutes. Private Robert Moore of Company G wrote in his diary that "orders came for us about 4½ P.M. to double-quick up to the field of battle and were [sic] very near run down when we got there. We made a charge through the woods as soon as we got to the battlefield & formed a line of battle."

Hoping to get more men, Evans sent to General R.L. Wright, asking him to muster the Loudoun militia. Wright reported in person, but without troops. He told Evans that he was "unable to get his men to turn out, though there was a great number in town [Leesburg] and arms and ammunition were offered them." This was later hotly denied by the editor of the Leesburg *Democratic Mirror* (November 27, 1861):

> *The 21st had been appointed by the Quartermaster*
> *to meet in Leesburg the owners of wagons, and pay*

them for same, which attracted to town some very
worthy gentlemen, principally elderly men . . .
probably 200 of them. . . . We know that many of
these inquired anxiously for arms and ammunition
with which to fight, but could get neither. . . . If
arms were provided no one found out.

Although the Loudoun Militia failed to muster, there were several individuals who happened to be in the vicinity and joined the fight. In Jenifer's after action report he mentioned William Rogers, R.L. Hendrick of Mecklenberg, Virginia, and a Mr. Peters. George Washington Ball also picked up a musket and fought. The most daring and useful of these stray fighters was Elijah Viers White, of whom Jenifer later said, "I never witnessed more coolness and courage than this young gentleman displayed." Evans also praised him in his dispatch.

White was twenty-nine years old, married with two children. Five years earlier he had purchased a 300-acre farm upstream from Ball's Bluff near Conrad's Ferry. Tall, slim, with high cheekbones and drooping eyelids, he had been born near Poolesville, Maryland, and had for awhile attended Granville College in Ohio, but he had dropped out of school to join a group of hot-blooded pro-slavery men bound for Kansas at a time when, as the Rev. Henry Ward Beecher is said to have put it, a Sharps rifle was a greater moral force than the Bible.* When the Civil War began, White joined first the local militia and then an irregular cavalry unit under Turner Ashby. Later in the war he was to organize his own band of irregulars who called themselves "Comanches."

It is not quite clear what White was doing back in Loudoun County in October 1861, or why he spent the night of the 20th with his neighbor, Henry Ball, instead of in his own

---

*Rifles and muskets smuggled into Kansas were known as "Beecher's Bibles."

house, but early on the morning of the 21st he set out for Leesburg in a buggy with Henry Ball's daughter, Kate, leaving his own horse in Ball's stable. He had not driven far when he heard the sounds of musketry—Duff's company skirmishing with Devens's men. He at once wheeled the buggy about and dashed back to the Ball farm; he dumped Kate, saddled his horse, and rode for the battlefield. The absence of a uniform did not distinguish these civilians from the soldiers. None of the 17th Mississippi had been issued uniforms as yet, and probably there were other troops who also fought in civilian clothes.

Perhaps it should be mentioned that among Eppa Hunton's "brave boys" in the 8th Virginia when they went into action there was also a 19-year-old girl—or so Loreta Janeta Velazquez later claimed.

According to a story she told a decade after the war, she was born in Havana, Cuba, in 1842, and was educated in New Orleans. At the age of 13 she was clandestinely married to an American army officer and by him had three children before she was 18. A romantic girl who did not hesitate to say, "I wish I had been created a man instead of a woman," she was fond of posing in front of a mirror dressed as a man, and she dreamed of becoming an American Joan of Arc. By the time the Civil War broke out her three children had died, and she persuaded her husband to give up his commission and join the Confederate army. She also tried to persuade him to allow her to go to war as one of his soldiers. When he would not consent, she claimed to have disguised herself as a Confederate officer, recruited 235 men in Arkansas and marched them to Pensacola, where she turned them over to her husband. Shortly thereafter, her husband was accidently killed.

C.J. Worthington, a former U.S. naval officer who knew her after the war, described her as "rather slender, somewhat above middle height, has more than average good looks, is quick and energetic in her movements and is very vivacious in conversation." In June 1861, dressed as a Confederate officer, calling herself Lieutenant Harry T. Buford, she acquired a "smart and mannerly" slave named "Bob" in Montgomery, Alabama, and then made her way to Virginia, where, she said, she took part in the battle of First Manassas (Bull Run). She found that "there is a positive enjoyment in the deadly perils of the occasion that nothing can equal."

After this battle, she moved to Leesburg, where she tried unsuccessfully to obtain an appointment from Colonel Evans. In spite of this disappointment, she claimed to have been on hand when the battle of Ball's Bluff opened and to have gone into the field with Hunton and his 8th Virginia. "Shortly after the fight began," she said, "I took charge of a company which had lost all its officers." According to her account, her slave, Bob, acquired a musket during the fight and also took part in the battle, making her "proud of the darky's pluck and enthusiasm." This, if true, would mean that there was a black on each side at Ball's Bluff.

The story told by Loreta Velazquez seems improbable and is uncorroborated, but improbable things happen in war, and women have been known successfully to pass as soldiers in other battles and in other wars. Perhaps she was there.

6.
Baker

✳ ✳ ✳

It was shortly after two o'clock in the afternoon when Baker and his horse finally crossed over to Virginia and he made his way to the top of Ball's Bluff. He was in good spirits. He bowed politely to Colonel Lee and said, "I congratulate you, sir, on the prospect of a battle." Lee returned his bow and said, "I suppose you assume command." Baker asked if he had held this position since daybreak. Lee said that he had, and Baker told him, "It shall receive honorable mention, sir." He then turned to the men of the 20th Massachusetts strung along the edge of the bluff and called out in his fine voice, "Boys, you want to fight, don't you?" The soldiers gave him a cheer and yelled that they did. "Then you shall have a chance," he promised.

Baker now rearranged his troops. Devens was out in front on the far side of the woods in a good position behind the heavy rail fence with an open field of fire. Had Baker moved all of his force forward to support him, the outcome of the battle might have been quite different, but he did not even go forward to inspect his position; instead, when Devens came back to confer with him, Baker ordered the 15th Massachusetts back onto the right of the new line he was forming in the open field in front of the bluff, and they moved into a chevron-shaped formation facing west and south. On the left he put the companies of the Tammany regiment, which were just making their appearance on the field. From right to left the line consisted of the 15th Massachusetts, the 20th Massachusetts, the 1st California and the Tammany Regiment. The rifled 6-pounder was placed on the left flank of the 20th Massachusetts and the two howitzers on their right flank.

Devens did not object to Baker's orders; he was happy to be relieved of the responsibilities that had been so unexpectedly thrust upon him. When he had learned that Baker had at last arrived on the field, he had turned to Major John Kimball and said, "Thank Heaven he has come. We have been waiting eight hours." Devens later described his feelings to a congressional committee: "I had a very strong feeling of relief, of course, because I knew that from that moment I had nothing to do but fight my regiment; I had nothing to do with the tactics of the battle, or with anything except the minor tactics."

In a letter to Dr. Oliver Wendell Holmes, Second Lieutenant Charles A. Whittier described the position of the 20th Massachusetts: "Here we were in the open field and the rebels all out of sight completely protected, nothing to cover us. Behind us a bank going to the river, abrupt, rocky woods. . . ." Baker posted a reserve of four companies in the center in such a position that they could only shoot down their own men while at the same time they were so near the firing line and so exposed in the open field that they came under a galling fire from the Confederates.

Baker showed his friend Wistar the message from Stone which estimated that the enemy were 4,000 strong. Wistar was inclined to agree that there must be at least that many. "We are certainly outnumbered in front," he said. "Yes," Baker agreed, "that is a bad condition of things." He had no thought of withdrawing, however, and he asked Wistar to "come and go around with me and look at my dispositions and plans, and say what you think of them." Wistar did not express any opinion, but he asked if he could extend his own regiment to the left. Baker told him, "I throw the entire responsibility for the left wing upon you. Do as you like."

Baker also asked Colonel Lee how he liked the dispositions that had been made. Lee answered only that he thought the main battle would be on the left of the line.

When Colonel Milton Cogswell, the only senior professional officer, arrived on the field with his Tammany Regiment, Baker, in high good humor, greeted him with a paraphrase of lines from Walter Scott's *The Lady of the Lake*:

> *One blast upon your bugle horn*
> *Is worth a thousand men—*

He asked Cogswell as well what he thought of the dispositions he had made. These questions to subordinates may have reflected Baker's uncertainty, but he appears to have been looking more for praise than criticism. Cogswell, however, looked around with his professional eyes and sniffed his disapproval. He pointed out that the wooded hill beyond the ravine on the left commanded his whole position and warned that if the Confederates occupied it, Baker would be destroyed. He recommended an immediate advance of the entire force to hold the hill. Baker ignored this good advice and told Cogswell to take charge of the artillery; he did not, however, say what he wanted done with it.

Twenty minutes later, skirmishers of the 8th Virginia occupied the hill beyond the ravine and opened a hot fire. Cogswell turned the guns on them, but the Virginians were too well protected by the trees and his fire was ineffectual. After only a few rounds the gunners were swept away by the musketry of Hunton's brave boys. Then Cogswell, Baker and some of the staff officers tried to man the gun, but it was a futile exercise, and to the troops the sight of the commanding officer and his staff performing as cannoneers was neither edifying nor inspiring.

Baker and Cogswell abandoned the guns and crossed over to the left of the line of infantry. They found Wistar was wounded, blood running down his beard and dripping onto his chest. One bullet had hit his jaw and a second had passed through his thigh near the scar of a wound he had received in his youth from an Indian's arrow in Oregon. Baker looked at him and seemed bemused: "The bullets are seeking for you but avoiding me," he said.

Wistar grimly cut a hole in his boot to let the blood run out and, in spite of his condition, rose to his feet to command his regiment. His line was becoming disorganized. When Baker ordered him to send out two companies of skirmishers, he protested, "The enemy cannot be less than 5,000 men, and probably 7,000 in front and around this field, and to send out two companies of skirmishers will be to sacrifice them."

"I cannot help it," Baker told him. "I must know what is there." Reluctantly, Wistar sent out two companies under Captain John Markoe. The Virginians quickly drove them back.

A third bullet struck Wistar in the right elbow, shattering all the bones and the joint, a wound so painful that it caused a momentary confusion and blurred his sight. Nevertheless, he bent down and with his left hand groped for his fallen sword, finally seizing it with a handful of bloody grass. When he straightened up, Baker grasped him by both shoulders and said, "What, Wistar, hit again?"

"Yes, I am afraid badly this time," Wistar replied, and he asked Baker to replace his sword in its scabbard for him. As he did so, Baker called out to a soldier, "Here, my man, catch hold of Colonel Wistar and get him to the boat somehow, if you have to carry him."

Baker may have been weak on tactics, but he was strong on words, and his talent for extemporaneous speech did not desert him. "The officer who dies with his men will never be harshly judged," he observed to one officer. Striding about the field, naked sword in hand, the other thrust into the breast of his coat a la Napoleon, he called out ringingly to the men of the 20th Massachusetts, "lie down" or "lie close." One soldier cried out, "But you don't lie close."

"No, my son," said Baker grandly, "and when you get to be a United States senator you will not lie down either."

Captain Louis Beirel of the California Regiment called, "General, won't you come out of the fire and stand behind my men?"

Feigning irritation, Baker barked, "Captain Beirel, do you attend to Company G. I will look after myself."

Men were falling on all sides now, and the sound of the musketry became a roar. Captain John Putnam of the 20th Massachusetts was hit in his right arm; later it would be amputated at the shoulder. Lieutenant Colonel George Ward of the 15th Massachusetts was hit in the left leg, the bullet passing through sideways, shattering the bones in a shocking manner. A private in the 20th Massachusetts saw a Confederate officer on a white horse and drew a bead on him, but found he could not pull the trigger. Lowering his musket, he stared at his right hand: his trigger finger had been shot away.

The heavy fighting had been in progress for an hour when young Oliver Wendell Holmes, Jr. was hit. He was in front of his company, calling encouragement, when a spent ball knocked the wind out of him. He crawled a few paces to the rear and tried to rise. Colonel Lee passed by and said, "That's right, Mr. Holmes. Go to the rear." But Holmes recovered and, getting to his feet, ran forward, flourishing his sword. Then a bullet struck his chest, "I felt as if a horse had kicked me and went over," he said later. First Sergeant Henry Smith (the artist who later deserted) seized Holmes and carried him to the rear. The bullet had passed almost completely through his body. Sergeant Smith squeezed it out and presented it to him. Holmes later recalled his thoughts and feelings:

Well—I remember the sickening feeling of water in my face—I was quite faint—and seeing poor Sgt.

95

[John] Merchant lying near—shot through the head and covered with blood—and then the thinking began. (Meanwhile hardly able to speak—at least coherently.) Shot through the lungs? Let's see—and I spit. Yes—already the blood was in my mouth. At once my thoughts jumped to "Children of the New Forest" (by Marryat) which I was fond of reading as a little boy, and in which the father of one of the heroines is shot through the lungs by a robber. I remember he died with terrible haemorrhages & great agony. What should I do? Just then I remembered and felt in my waist coat pocket—Yes there it was—a little bottle of laudanum which I had brought along. But I won't take it yet; no, see a doctor first. It may not be as bad as it looks. At any rate wait until the pain begins—

Holmes was helped to the bottom of the bluff, where the scow had just left with a load of wounded, leaving only a small metallic boat on the shore. Semi-conscious he heard another man groan and asked himself, "Now wouldn't Sir Philip Sydney have that other feller put into the boat first?" But without protest he allowed himself to be hauled aboard and carried over to Harrison's Island.

The Confederates were also taking casualties. Many years later, when Elijah White was an old man, he wrote: "In visions now I see those brave fellows falling like leaves in autumn before the northern blast." A volley from the California Regiment mortally wounded Colonel Burt of the 18th Mississippi almost as soon as he brought his regiment onto the field. As he was being lowered from his horse, he turned to an aide and said in a quiet, conversational tone: "Go tell Colonel Jenifer I am wounded and shall have to leave the field."

Experienced commanders in nineteenth-century armies often issued stern orders before a battle that the wounded must be left untended; punishment was threatened for those who left off fighting to help a wounded comrade. However, no such orders had been issued to the Union troops at Ball's Bluff, and Captain Francis Young told of the result: "A great many of our men became disheartened and frightened and whenever anyone was hit, six or seven would take hold of him and carry him away."

Officers on both sides behaved with great coolness under fire. Captain William Bartlett, commanding Company I of the 20th Massachusetts, walked about calmly among his men, who were lying prone on the ground, and joked with them. Seeing First Lieutenant George Macy of Nantucket lying where the grass was turned up, he teased him, saying he should be careful or he would get his coat stained. For awhile he stood talking to Second Lieutenant Henry Abbott (called "Little" or "Lit" by his friends) and two or three times he turned and said to him, "Why Lit, aren't you hit yet?" Abbott remained untouched. Nineteen years old, he had been a student at Harvard when the war began; he was to live another year and a half and be promoted to major before falling mortally wounded at the Battle of the Wilderness.

Coolness under fire is always feigned, for no man remains truly calm while being shot at. But it is helpful for soldiers, particularly officers, to appear so, for it tends to keep fighting men to their bloody task, and in the nineteenth century it was almost the only purpose served by junior officers on a battlefield. Such coolness requires bravery, of course, and bravery is always inspiring. Accounts of eye witnesses differ as to the degree of calm exhibited by Baker on the field. Colonel Lee loyally testified that "his bearing was that of a cool, gallant and chivalric officer," but Lieutenant Church Howe said he was "much excited at the time." Of Baker's bravery there is no doubt, but the picture that emerges is that of a man in a state of euphoria.

He saw himself, it seems, as the heroic leader, issuing orders, shouting encouragement in his beautiful, melodic voice, and striking poses. He was an actor playing a real life role and, like all actors, he sought the approval of his audience. Perhaps the roar of musketry sounded as sweet to him as the roar of the crowds he had pleased, but here the sound was the voice of death; those men falling were ripped and torn by bullets. The blood was real, but for Ned Baker, striding about through the swirling, pungent smoke of battle with his naked sword, it was simply grand. This was the greatest moment in his life, and he revelled in it. One can regard his posturing as amusing or noble, but one thing mars either of these conceptions: the orders he gave and those he failed to give were alike disastrous.

To an aide Baker commented jocularly on the enemy's marksmanship saying that they meant well enough but did not seem to hit much. To Colonel Devens's men he called out: "If I had two more such regiments as the Massachusetts 15th I would cut my way to Leesburg!" Seeing a Confederate officer on a horse, he shouted: "There is General Johnston! Fire, boys, fire!" It was not Johnston, of course, but a rumor spread among the Confederates that General Joseph Johnston, then in command of the Army of Northern Virginia, had arrived on the field to take personal command.

Captain Francis Young, an aide to Colonel Baker, was later to tell a congressional committee a curious story. He testified that in the middle of the battle Captain Charles Stewart, Stone's assistant adjutant general (i.e. chief of staff), appeared on the field and said to him: "Tell Colonel Baker that General Gorman is coming up on the left from Edwards Ferry with 5,000 men."

Captain Stewart's given name was Adolphus Frederick Charles William Vane-Tempest; he was the third son of the 3rd Marquis of Londonberry and a former officer in the Scots Fusilier Guards who had fought in the Crimea. He was not a popular officer, and Major J.J. Dimmick of the 2nd New York Militia said of him: "He is a very supercilious fellow, and has insulted every officer who has gone there [Stone's headquarters]. He gets beastly drunk two or three times a week."

Captain Young apparently did not like Stewart, for when the message was delivered, Young snapped, "Go and tell him yourself."

"I deliver the order to you as his aide," Stewart replied.

There is no evidence other than Captain Young's testimony that such an improbable message was sent, though Stewart did indeed arrive on the field. If Stone sent any message of importance, he would most probably have written it, and Stewart would have delivered the message directly to Baker. As will be seen, Young's testimony was not unbiased and must be accepted with caution. If Stewart did deliver a message, Young must certainly have misunderstood it. At the time he was busy trying to root out some skulkers from behind trees and rocks and get them back into the firing line. In any case, he passed on the message as he understood it to Baker, who then went up and down the line calling, "Stand fast, boys! We are going to have reinforcements. General Gorman is coming up with 5,000 men. We will beat them yet!"

Whether as a result of Young's message or a conclusion he reached independently, Baker did seem to think that help was on the way. When a captain of the California Regiment reported Confederates moving up a ravine on the left, Baker was undisturbed: "No doubt they are General Gorman's men coming up from Edwards Ferry."

It became increasingly obvious that Baker's force was getting the worst of the exchange of musketry, and about five o'clock Baker called Captain Young to his side and said, "You had better go down to Stone and tell him we are fixed."

Young, who seemed to make a habit of disobeying orders and talking back to his superiors, replied, "Colonel, I suppose he knows that as well as you do."

"I command you to go for reinforcements," Baker snapped.

Young made his way over the brow of the bluff and part of

"Colonel Baker is killed!" Several Rebels dashed out of the woods and one of them, a big red-head, fired at Baker four or five times at close

range. The red-head was killed (see following page) in the ensuing scramble for the body.

the way down, but when he saw that there were no boats on the Virginia shore, he started back. Just then he heard someone shout, "Colonel Baker is killed!"

Baker had been walking in front of his men on the left of the Union line when a group of Confederate soldiers dashed out of the woods and a big, red-headed man in his shirt sleeves, armed with a revolver, aimed and fired at him four or five times. Baker died instantly. Several Confederates rushed to get possession of the body, or at least his sword, but Frederick Harvey, adjutant of the California Regiment, cried out, "For God's sake, boys, are you going to let them have the general's body?" At this, several officers and men sprang forward, and Captain Louis Beiral of the California Regiment shot the red-haired Confederate who had killed Baker. Captain Young, Captain Robert Hicks, and Baker's nephew, Second Lieutenant Edward Jerome, carried the corpse off the field. Young and Jerome got the body down the bluff and onto a flatboat filled with dead and wounded.

Baker's body was carried over the bluff and then ferried to Harrison's Island. When the corpse was carried slowly from the boat, troops waiting to cross to the battle fell silent, demoralized by the sight.

When Baker's body was taken off the boat on Harrison's Island, soldiers from the 19th Massachusetts stood on the shore waiting to cross. They had been standing inactive for some time, watching the dead and wounded being lifted from the boats and carried past them. The sight of the wounded, their arms, legs and heads tied up in bloody bandages or their wounds still open and exposed had its effect on the nervous young men awaiting their turn to experience their first battle. When Baker's body was taken from the boat and slowly carried away, there was a hush along the line. "This incident had a most demoralizing affect," wrote one soldier.

The battle was over before the 19th Massachusetts could join the fight, but at dusk, while the battle still raged, some of them were called upon to pole the scow back and forth between the island and the Virginia shore, and these men recovered their spirits and sang as they poled: "We'll Hang Jeff Davis to a Sour Apple Tree." The singing died down shortly, for the Union forces were on the verge of disaster.

While things were falling apart at Ball's Bluff, Stone was under the impression that operations there were progressing nicely. Both he and McClellan were beginning to think in grander terms. Early in the afternoon McClellan had telegraphed to ask the size of the Confederate force engaged and to offer Stone more troops if he needed them. He also asked, "What force in your opinion would it require to carry Leesburg? Answer at once, as I may require you to take it today; and, if so, I will support you on the other side of the river from Darnestown." Stone, still under the impression that McCall was at Dranesville, only twelve miles from Goose Creek and unaware that McClellan had forgotten to inform him that he had withdrawn this force, replied that he thought Evans had 4,000 men and four or more guns and added, "I believe this command can occupy Leesburg to-day. We are a little short of boats."

"We are a little short of boats"—was to be one of the greatest understatements of the war.

7.
Battle's End
✳✳✳

It was about the time that Devens's men were falling back to their final position at the top of the bluff that McClellan telegraphed in code: "Take Leesburg." Stone, unable to read the message because he lacked the key, telegraphed back: "I have the box but not the key." Under the impression that Stone was referring to an actual box, McClellan sent Lieutenant Colonel Richard B. Irving, an assistant adjutant general, to Stone's home in Washington to ask for its key.

The telegrams that afternoon from Stone at Edwards Ferry to McClellan in Washington gave no hint of disaster. At 4:00 P.M. Stone reported: "Nearly all my force across the river. Baker on the right, Gorman on the left. Right sharply engaged." Bad news began at 6:45 P.M. when Stone wired: "Colonel Baker has been killed at the head of his brigade. I go to the right at once." This was the message Lincoln read at McClellan's headquarters. At 9:45 P.M. Stone telegraphed: "I deeply regret to report a repulse on the right after Colonel Baker's death. I have called on General Banks for more troops. The enemy were re-enforced at the time of confusion, and our loss is severe. We still hold Harrison's Island. . . ."

On Ball's Bluff after Baker's death Colonel Lee assumed that he was the senior officer and in command. Devens, too, thought Lee was the next senior officer and reported to him. Lee expressed the opinion that the battle was utterly lost and that the only thing to be done was to retreat to the river, but before he could give any orders Colonel Cogswell appeared and insisted that he was entitled to the command. Lee and

Devens gave way and Cogswell announced his determination to fight his way to Edwards Ferry. Indeed, this was the only practical thing to do. Devens was ordered to bring his regiment from the right flank to the left preliminary to joining in a charge. Cogswell returned to his own Tammany Regiment and called out, "Boys, we will cut our way through to Edwards Ferry!"

It was shortly after this, when the sun had set and twilight fallen, that an officer appeared in front of the Tammany Regiment, waving his hat and calling on the soldiers to charge. Several companies of New Yorkers sprang forward. The 15th Massachusetts also advanced, but Devens leaped in front of his regiment on the left of his line and ordered them back: "For God's sake, men, stand firm where you are!" At once he was seconded by Major John Kimball on the right of the line, and the regiment held its ground. The handful of Tammany men who charged were shot to pieces. It was later believed that it was not a Union but a Confederate officer who had ordered the charge.

The story of the Confederate officer who led a Union charge was often repeated during and after the war, and it lost nothing in the telling. Some came to believe it was really a phantom,

A Union bayonet charge into heavy Rebel fire.

a creature from the spirit world, who deliberately led the Tammany boys to their deaths. To this day, boys and girls in Loudoun County avoid the Ball's Bluff battlefield at night, for although it seems an ideal place for lovers, being tucked away at the end of a dead-end road, many believe the place is haunted by the phantom.

Elijah White many years after the war positively identified the Confederate officer as Lieutenant Charles B. Wildman, who was serving on Evans's staff that day. Eppa Hunton of the 8th Virginia, perhaps accepting White's word, also said that Wildman was the mysterious officer. Said Hunton: "He was a gallant, fine fellow, but addicted to intemperance." White added that Wildman was too drunk to know what he was doing that day. There is reason to believe, however, that Lieutenant Wildman's name has been unjustly blackened. In his after action report, Evans singled out Wildman for special commendation: "Lieutenant Wildman conducted the Eighteenth Regiment . . . to their . . . positions in the action, and repeatedly bore my orders under heavy fire." This does not sound like the actions of a man so drunk he could not tell his own troops from the enemy's.

There is solid evidence for absolving Wildman. A close reading of the record and a comparison of times and places leads to the inevitable conclusion that there was no Confederate officer leading the Tammany Regiment—and no phantom either. Colonel Cogswell was taken prisoner, and it was not until a year after the battle that he was able to submit his after action report. By then the war had moved on to bigger, more ferocious battles; Stone, who received the report, no longer had a command and was involved with disturbing problems of his own. So Cogswell's words were largely ignored, but this is what he had to say:

Having given these orders [for the break out
towards Edwards Ferry] I proceeded to the front,
and finding our lines pressed severely, I ordered an

*advance of the whole force on the right of the en-
emy line. I was followed by the remnants of my
two companies and a portion of the California regiment, but, for some reason unknown to me, was
not joined by either the Fifteenth or the Twentieth
Massachusetts Regiments.*

Although it seems a shame to discredit an extraordinary
story, it would appear that the officer who ordered the charge
was neither a Confederate officer nor a Pied-Piper style phantom, but the luckless Milton Cogswell.

It was about six o'clock in the evening when Cogswell
launched his abortive charge in the twilight, the last con-
vulsive twitch of the Union forces on Ball's Bluff. Then the
Confederates' final attack went in. Lieutenant Colonel John
McGuirk of the 17th Mississippi described it:

*The men manifested confidence under the coolness
of their officers. They seemed fighting a sham battle, when above the roar of musketry was heard the
command of Colonel Featherston, "Charge Missis-
sippians! Charge! Drive them into the Potomac or
into eternity!" The sound of his voice seemed to
echo from the vales of Maryland. The line arose as
one man from a kneeling posture, discharged a
deadly volley, advanced the crescent line, and then
encircled the invaders.*

Elijah White galloped in front of the charging Confederates
and called, "Follow me! I'll show you the way!" A soldier of
the 20th Massachusetts, sheltering behind a tree, aimed at
him and fired, then threw away his musket and fled. *

---

*Thirty-two years later, when White was showing a group of veterans
of the 20th Massachusetts over the battlefield, he heard one man tell of
firing this shot, ending his story with, "I don't know whether I killed
him or not." "No, thank God, you did not," said White.

The wounded Lieutenant Colonel Wistar was being carried from the field when he heard an officer, probably Captain Henry Tremlett, call out, "Company A, 20th Massachusetts, retreat to the ferry!", a call quickly echoed by other officers to their companies. The Union line broke. Soldiers tumbled over the edge of the bluff and dashed down to the riverside in a confused mob. Panic gripped them. Screams filled the air as the men leaped over the bluff, sometimes onto the heads or bayonets of those below them. A grey-haired private of the California Regiment had his head smashed on the rocks by the boots of a New Yorker who leaped on him—and broke his neck in the fall.

Captain Francis Young later tried to describe the scene for readers of the San Francisco *Herald*: "Tumbling down the steep heights; the enemy following, murdering, and taking prisoners. . . . Hundreds plunged into the rapid current, and the shrieks of the drowning added to the horror. . . . All was terror, confusion and dismay." The last loads from Harrison's Island to the Virginia shore had brought a company of the Tammany Regiment commanded by Captain T.H. O'Meara. Although their comrades were in full retreat, O'Meara and his men stormed up the bluff and opened fire at the Confederates.

Captain William Bartlett and Lieutenant Charles Peirson helped Colonel Lee down the bluff: Peirson took his left arm and Bartlett his right. In a letter to his mother four days later, Bartlett described what he saw on the river bank: "Here was a horrible scene. Men crowded together, the wounded and the dying. The water was full of human beings, struggling with each other and the water, the surface of which looked like a pond when it rains, from the withering volleys that the enemy were pouring down from the top of the bank."

There were too few boats for the panic-stricken men, desperate to cross the fifty feet of water that separated them from Harrison's Island and safety. Accounts of the number and

"Tumbling down the steep heights; the enemy following, murdering, and taking prisoners. . .Hundreds plunged into the rapid current, and the shrieks of the drowning added to the horror. . .All was terror, confusion and dismay."—Captain Francis Young.

kinds of boats differ, but it seems probable that when the rout began there were only two skiffs, a 25-foot flatboat, a scow, and a four-oared metallic boat. The Rev. Scanlon, chaplain of the 15th Massachusetts, tried manfully, without much success, to reserve the boats for the wounded. The flatboat, which could conveniently carry forty-five men, if necessary 65, set out from the Virginia shore loaded with nearly a hundred soldiers, fit as well as wounded. It had gone only about fifteen feet when it capsized. Only one man is known to have survived.

Lieutenant William Coulter of the 15th Massachusetts saw the boat go down: "This was a terrible sight. . . . But a few moments before this I had stood on the battle-ground and witnessed a score or more of brave men fall by the bullet, but I was not so much affected as I was when I saw that boat go down with its living freight."

The metallic boat floated, empty, down the river when the man bringing it back from Harrison's Island was shot. The skiffs seemed to disappear. It became a question of swim or die, for no one on the Union side tried to surrender and, oddly enough, none of the Confederates demanded it. Standing on the top of the bluff, they fired down on the dark masses of men huddled along the riverside and at those swimming in the water.

The swimmers seemed to come under a particularly heavy fire, perhaps because they could be seen more clearly. One soldier wrote that the river was churned into a froth "as white as in a great hail storm" by the bullets. Lieutenant Colonel McGuirk noted that some Union soldiers became so terrified that they turned around and swam back, even when they were more than half way across. Loreta Velasque described her feelings (perhaps imagined) as she watched the men being shot in the water:

> All the woman in me revolted at the fiendish delight which some of our soldiers displayed at the sight of the terrible agony endured by those who had, but a short time before, been contesting the field with them so valiantly. . . . I was sick with horror; and as the cold shivering ran through me, and my heart stood still in my bosom, I shut my eyes for a moment, wishing that it was all over, but only to open them again to gaze on a spectacle that had a terrible fascination for me, in spite of its horror.

The Union officers ordered all that could swim to do so, but first to throw their muskets in the river. Many were reluctant to part with their weapons. Lieutenant Norwood Hallowell of the 20th Massachusetts swam over with his sword hung about his neck. Captain Beiral tried to do this as well but was forced to drop his sword halfway across. The men who had been issued the prized rifled muskets were particularly reluctant to discard them, and many tried to swim with their guns tied to their backs; some succeeded. One man, unable to swim, hid for two days, then found a boat and returned to his regiment with his musket.

The possessions people are not willing to abandon to save their lives in moments of danger are many and varied, and often nearly inexplicable; often they are of symbolic rather than of intrinsic value. When the color sergeant of the California Regiment was shot through both legs early in the battle, the regimental flag was taken up by Private George Suttie who later tried to swim the river with it; in mid-stream cold and fatigue forced him to drop it and it floated away. Colonel Devens had no qualms about tossing his sword into the Potomac, but he was sorry to part with his coat, for it had on it a button that had been crushed by a bullet and he fancied wearing it as if it were a medal. Lieutenant Macy stripped himself naked except for his hat, which he kept because he carried a miniature of his fiancée inside it. Macy also tried to carry his sword, but was forced to drop it. Captain Caspar Crowninshield tried to save his watch, for which he had a sentimental attachment, by carrying it in his mouth. He had been stroke oar at Harvard and was a powerful swimmer, so he succeeded in reaching Harrison's Island and slept that night on a pile of straw with his watch beside him. In the morning he got up and walked off without it.

At least one man was more concerned with cash and comfort than with sentiment. An Irishman in Company D, 15th Massachusetts, threw off his coat and pants and successfully swam through the stiff current and the hail of bullets to the island; then he remembered that he had left $18.25 in the pocket of his coat, along with his pipe, and he swam back to retrieve them. When a newspaper reporter, hearing of the feat, asked him about it, he explained: "Oh, yes sir, 'twas all I'd saved from my three months' service, and I'm very fond of me pipe." Captain Philbrick successfully swam across with his money in his mouth. Others who tried to save their money were less fortunate. A Confederate soldier who reported finding the body of a Union officer with $126 in gold in his pockets, reflected that "it had cost his life."

The whole surface of the river between the island and the Virginia shore was covered with struggling, frightened men, many crying out for help. The weak reached out to the strong and sometimes dragged them down. A Captain of the California Regiment was found dead with two men clutching his neckboard. Alois Babo and Reinhold Wesselhoeft, lieutenants in Captain Dreher's German company of the 20th Massachusetts, entered the water together without taking off any of their clothes, not even their shoes, and began to swim. One was heard to exclaim in German that he was shot. Neither was ever seen alive again. Thirteen days after the battle Lieutenant Wesselhoeft's body, bearing no wounds, was found washed up on the shore. It was assumed that he had drowned trying to save his friend.

Captain O'Meara swam to the island and searched frantically for a boat. Unable to find one, he swam back to share the fate of his men. When Lieutenant Hallowell arrived on Harrison's Island, he downed a shot of brandy, borrowed a shirt and a pair of drawers, and set out to see what he could do to help the others. He found several men from his regiment, one of whom thought he knew the whereabouts of a rowboat on the Maryland side of the island. Hallowell dispatched a party to get it, and when the boat was eventually brought around he sent it over to the foot of the bluff. There Captain O'Meara took charge of it and sent back a load of wounded. Several trips were made and some thirty or forty men were saved. Having successfully established this little ferry service, Hallowell put some men to work making a raft of fence rails fastened together with belts. This he poled over to the Virginia shore. He picked up three men and started back, but just before he reached the island the belts broke and the raft fell apart. Only Hallowell and one other escaped. The 19th Massachusetts was on the island, and one of its men found a small boat in which he successfully made three trips back and forth, saving about fifteen or twenty men.

Second Lieutenant Richard Derby, Company H, 15th Massachusetts, was so confident that he could easily swim across to the island that he did not bother to take off his clothes or even to empty his pockets. He found a board and laid on it his boots, sword and pistol. "I was anxious to save my sword," he said, "as it looked too much like surrendering to lose that. . . . I pushed off quite deliberately, although the water was full of drowning soldiers and bullets from the rebels on the top of the bluff. I made slow progress with one hand, and had to abandon my raft and cargo. I got along very well a little more than half-way, when I found that every effort I made only pushed my head under water, and suddenly it flashed upon me that I should drown. I didn't feel any pain or exhaustion—the sensation was exactly like being overcome with drowsiness. I swallowed water in spite of all I could do, till at last I sank unconscious. There was a small island near Harrison's against which the current drifted me, and aroused me enough to crawl a step or two, but not enough to know what I was doing till I dropped just by the edge of the water with my head in the soft clay-mud."[*]

Derby later made an inventory of all that he was carrying on his person when he entered the water: knife, fork, spoon, horn pocket comb, large jack knife, a half pound of gold and

---

[*]This island, clearly shown on maps of the period, is now joined to Harrison's Island.

silver coins, a package of envelopes, a large memorandum book, a handful of bullets, a metallic box of caps, a flask of powder, a watch, and, of course, all his clothes.

Lieutenant Charles Eager, also of the 15th Massachusetts, could not swim, but three of his men offered to carry him across. Eager refused, fearing he would drown them all. However, they were confident and insistent, so he at last agreed to try if they could find some wood for him to hang onto. A tree limb ten feet long and six inches thick and a floor joist of about the same length were found and on these Eager said he was willing to set forth alone. The point was still being argued when a fourth soldier, Walter Eames, offered to help.

Just as they were about to push off, Colonel Devens came to the water's edge. He had taken off his equipment and some of his clothes, but he did not know how to swim. Eames called out to him: "Hop on our craft and we will take you across too." Devens hesitated for a moment and then plunged in. The current was stronger than any of them had expected and the four soldiers swimming had great difficulty struggling against it. They almost failed. They were carried rapidly downstream, but finally came ashore on the little island where Lieutenant Derby lay. They plucked him from the mud, then waded across the waist-deep strip of water that separated them from Harrison's Island. Two days later, Lieutenant Eager bragged to his wife, Libbie: "I came over with all my equipments [sic] revolver etc. & I guess I am the only one that done it." He neglected to mention the men who helped him accomplish this feat.

Colonel Lee was not so fortunate. Accompanied by his adjutant, Charles Peirson; his assistant surgeon, Edward H.R. Revere; First Lieutenant George Perry and a few enlisted men, Lee started north along the shore. They stopped once and tried to make a raft of fence rails tied together with belts, but the raft sank. Further north they came to Smart's Mill, and there a Black showed them a sunken skiff in the millrace. He was given a $10 gold piece for his trouble, but Lee decided that there was not time to repair the boat, so they abandoned it and pressed on. Soon after they ran into a Confederate picket and were forced to surrender.

Captain Bartlett and Lieutenant Abbott could both swim, but they elected to remain with the men who could not. "Lit" Abbott gave his watch to a soldier named Kelly, "the bravest boy in our company," and asked him to take it to his mother in Boston and tell her that her son was probably a prisoner. Bartlett rounded up two other officers of the 20th Massachusetts—Captain Henry Tremlett and Lieutenant Charles Whittier—some forty men from the two Massachusetts regiments, and about an equal number of men from the Tammany Regiment and led them on the same path taken by Colonel Lee. At Smart's Mill the same Black showed them the sunken skiff. This time he was given $5.

Unlike Lee, Bartlett thought something could be done with the skiff. He ordered it lifted out and carried down to the river. A few minor repairs made it serviceable enough to carry five men, so Bartlett organized a shuttle. Lieutenant Whittier was sent over with the second load to take charge of the men and to make sure that the skiff was sent back. Tremlett, Abbott and Bartlett crossed last. By nine o'clock, three hours after the retreat began, all were safe on Harrison's Island.

Captain Charles Watson of the 15th Massachusetts led eight men in the opposite direction and, keeping close to the shore, reached the safety of Gorman's lines at Edwards Ferry.

Some of the soldiers safe on Harrison's Island, hearing the cries of the wounded from across the water and the frantic pleas for boats, railed against their helplessness. Not everyone shared this feeling. Lieutenant James Dodge, Company E, 19th Massachusetts, spied some men running away from the river bank toward the Maryland side of the island. He called out to them to stop, but they ignored him until he threatened to shoot. They had crossed over from the Virginia shore in a small boat, but in spite of Dodge's order and threats, they refused to row back and rescue their comrades. Two of Dodge's own men heroically manned the boat and made three trips across the river, rescuing fifteen men. "But of this number," said Dodge, "not one could be found who would return for their comrades."

The Confederates made no determined effort to complete their victory. As night fell, the 17th and 18th Mississippi regiments drew back from the river and bivouacked in an open field near Leesburg, leaving only two companies under Lieutenant Colonel McGuirk to stand guard. Colonel Hunton ordered his 8th Virginia to Fort Evans, detailing Lieutenant Charles Berkeley and twelve men to stay behind on the field as a picket. At his request, Elijah White consented to stay with them.

Women in Leesburg hastened to send food out to them. Hunton, sick and exhausted, gratefully accepted a ride into town in the little spring wagon that Mr. John Smart had driven out to the battlefield. Hunton had had a hard day and there had been one bad moment when his horse, "old Morgan," ran away with him and he had lost his pistols and hat. "I feared," he said later, "that my brave boys would think it was I that was running."

Evans too was ready to call it quits. He had not actually appeared on the battlefield (in fact, there was later a quarrel among the Confederate colonels as to just who had been in command on the field), but "Shanks" Evans had really been responsible for it all. He had taken a tremendous risk when, gambling that Gorman would not advance from Edwards Ferry, he had sent nearly all his troops to Ball's Bluff, but it was a decision that had won him a brilliant victory. Elated, he left Fort Evans for Leesburg to celebrate with a few drinks— a few too many drinks according to the abstentious Hunton. But the final act of the drama had not yet been played.

During the night, Elijah White, scouting below the bluff,

encountered a Union soldier who challenged him. "Come here," White called. The soldier came closer. "Who are you?" White demanded.

"New York Tammany Regiment."

"You are my prisoner. Surrender."

The soldier lowered his rifle and bayonet. "Never to any man!"

White shot first and then crept back up the bluff. When word was sent back to Fort Evans that there were still large numbers of Union troops milling about below the bluff, Captain William Berkeley of the 8th Virginia called for volunteers and, guided by White, led a group of about forty officers and men back to the river to demand that they surrender. Many did. Berkeley marched 325 prisoners into Leesburg.

The battle over, several people from Leesburg and its environs came out onto the battlefield. Murphy Schumater, a farmer who lived five miles south of town, rode out to look for his 21-year-old son. Encountering a soldier covered with the grime and powder of battle, he drew in his horse and asked if he knew anything of Private Lewis Schumater of Captain Berkeley's Company C, 8th Virginia. The soldier laughed and Schumater bent down and peered into the smiling, powder-stained face of his son.

8.
In the Battle's Wake

✳ ✳ ✳

Battles are more than shooting and killing, winning or losing, more than the excitement and the fears, the bravery and the cowardice. Battles also involve the pain of the wounded and the dying, burial details, the sorrows of friends and relatives, the exaltation of the victors and the dismay of the defeated, the trials of those taken prisoner, the rewards and the recriminations; then too there are the reports, the reflections of cooled emotions, and all that men learned from the battle— or thought they had—and what they did because of the battle or because of what they thought about it. Each battle casts long shadows, and if battles' aftermaths lack the noise and the fury, the excitement and the glory, still, what is said and what is suffered afterwards, what is done and what is not done when the firing stops, is often more important and more enduring than the story of the conflict itself. In a sifting of the debris of battle one can find causes as well as effects, answers among the questions.

Battle is a furnace that smelts the ore of men's souls, and, in sorting through what remains after the battle's flames have been extinguished, some men see that they and many of their comrades are among the dross; they failed to live up to images of themselves which they previously entertained. Others feel that they have successfully met some unstated standard, that they have passed a crucial test; they discover that they have become tempered steel. Among the latter after Ball's Bluff was Oliver Wendell Holmes, Jr., who told his mother: "I felt and acted very cool and did my duty I am sure. . . . Whatever happens I am very happy in the conviction I did my duty."

Captain William Francis Bartlett had also proved himself a man to be numbered among the brave. And he discovered something more. Less than six months earlier he had been a 21-year-old student at Harvard—pleasure loving, not very industrious—with no fixed purpose in life. At Ball's Bluff he found that he was a resourceful leader of men; it was through his initiative and leadership that some eighty men had been able to escape. This discovery gave his life a purpose, and that purpose was to be a soldier. He was to have his fill of soldiering, and in the four years of civil war everything of importance in his life occurred. In the course of the war he married, knew victory and defeat, suffered imprisonment, knew the anguish of severe wounds, and emerged a 25-year-old major general, without a left leg (lost at Yorktown), with a withered arm and harboring germs in his bowels that would never go away.

There was a widely believed rumor that Shanks Evans had been in his tent drunk while the battle of Ball's Bluff was being fought. He may have taken a drink or two, but he was certainly not drunk. In any case, the laurels of the victor could not be denied him. He was promoted to the rank of brigadier general; his native South Carolina gave him a gold medal; and he found himself briefly a popular hero. A year earlier he had been an obscure cavalry captain; now, after distinguishing himself in two battles, he was a general. Doubtless it seemed to him, as it certainly appeared at the time, that he was on the threshold of a brilliant military career; but this was not to be, for although he was to fight in many more battles, his career reached its apogee at Ball's Bluff.

One whose future was inextricably tied to the Union catastrophe was General Charles Stone. He doubtless suspected this, but he could never have imagined the chain reaction of bizarre events in his life which the battle of Ball's Bluff would actuate. His first reactions, naturally enough, were surprise and shock, followed by a desire to know the extent of the disaster and the anxiety, normal and proper for his position, lest the Confederates follow up their victory by crossing the Potomac and attacking him in Maryland.

At first he had hoped that his troops could be rallied, that reinforcements would turn the tide; then the truth was brought home to him and he was appalled to learn the extent of the disaster. He had trouble explaining the defeat to McClellan and Lincoln, both of whom were trying to find out what had happened. Telegrams went flying back and forth all night. At 10:00 P.M. Lincoln telegraphed to the "Officer in Command at Poolesville":

> Send a mounted messenger to the battle ground and bring me information from General Stone. I want the particulars as to result of engagement and the relative position of the forces for the night, their numbers, and such other information as will give me a correct understanding of affairs.

To this, Stone gave an incomplete reply:

> It is impossible to give full particulars of what is yet inexplicable to me. Our troops under Colonel Baker were reported in good condition and position until fifteen minutes of the death of Colonel Baker. We have still possession of Harrison's Island and some 1,500 men on the Virginia side opposite Edwards Ferry; 600 more going over. We have lost several field officers, and Colonels Lee and Cogswell are said to be prisoners; Colonel Ward wounded. The enemy has not thus far attempted any attack on our positions. We have lost two

*mountain howitzers and one rifled James gun. The
enemy was undoubtedly re-enforced in the evening,
but how much it is impossible to say. The report of
killed made to me half an hour before the disaster
was 30. Our killed and wounded may reach 200;
number of prisoners unknown.*

On learning of Baker's death, Stone had hastily telegraphed
the news to Washington, then mounted his horse and started
down the towpath towards the scene of the tragedy. On his
way he encountered disheartening signs of the disaster that
had overtaken his troops—demoralized deserters, walking
wounded, wet and dispirited men who had swum the river.
He also came upon an ambulance carrying Baker's corpse with
Captain Francis Young and Lieutenant Edward Jerome es-
corting it. Lieutenant Edward Baker was probably in the party
as well.

The time was nine o'clock at night and Young now belatedly
delivered the message Baker had ordered him to take four
hours earlier, calling out, "For God's sake, General Stone,
send up reinforcements on the left." (He meant, presumably,
Gorman's brigade.) This was no way for a captain to talk to
a general, and Stone, irritated, asked, "Who are you, sir?"
Young apologized and Stone told him: "Take the best care of
Colonel Baker's body. Return to the field and you will be
reinforced." Young took the body first to Edwards Ferry and
then to Poolesville, where he turned the corpse over to an
undertaker. He then took it upon himself to telegraph president Lincoln, after which, instead of returning to his regiment, he went to bed.

Stone had initially considered withdrawing Gorman's brigade at Edwards Ferry lest it, too, be scuppered, but McClellan
ordered him to entrench and hold his position on the Virginia
shore "at all hazards."

At 11:00 P.M. Stone reported to McClellan:

> *We hold the ground half a mile back of Edwards Ferry, on Virginia shore. Harrison's Island has parts of thirteen companies, say 700 men, and will soon be re-enforced by 100 more fresh men, besides what support Hamilton brings.* * *I cover the shore opposite this with guns, and am disposing others to help the defense of Harrison's. I think the men will fight well. Entrenchments were ordered this morning.*

To this McClellan replied:

> *I repeat to you, under no circumstances abandon the Virginia shore, but entrench yourself and hold your own. If you can make your men fight you will be supported by General Banks.*

Stone, still thinking that McCall's division was at Dranesville, telegraphed at 11:30 P.M. to McClellan: "I strongly recommend that an advance towards Goose Creek be made from Dranesville to strike the right of the enemy." McClellan replied that this was impossible, but he omitted to tell Stone that McCall had withdrawn from Dranesville twelve hours earlier. At three o'clock in the morning Banks reached Edwards Ferry and, being senior to Stone, assumed command. Later in the day, in the middle of a gusty rainstorm, McClellan himself arrived from Washington.

There were about 1,600 Federal troops on the Virginia shore at Edwards Ferry, but not all of these were equipped to fight.

---

*Brigadier General Charles S. Hamilton commanded a brigade in Bank's division.

The 7th Michigan was armed with what was called the Belgian rifle, but was, in fact, a flintlock converted to percussion by the Belgian method of placing the nipple on the side rather than on the barrel. Captain John Richardson of that regiment described it as "a very good gun when we could get it off . . . but on an average we could not get them off without snapping four or five times." Captain John Patrick of the 30th Pennsylvania said he had known the gun to burst in the hands of men firing blank cartridges, adding that "of course the men do not feel very safe with such weapons." The 7th Michigan were given entrenching tools and told to dig; fortunately, they were not called upon to fight.

The Federals feared an attack in overwhelming numbers; so did the Confederates. Evans, after skirmishing a bit with Gorman's men on the 22nd, withdrew his force up Goose Creek to Carter's mill and dug in there. McClellan, after looking over the situation in person, ordered Stone to withdraw Gorman's brigade, and all contact between the opposing forces was broken off.

The situation on the upper Potomac on both sides of the river returned to much the same state that had existed before the battle, though there were still a number of alarms. The Leesburg *Democratic Mirror* (October 30) reported:

> *The past week has been one of unusual excitement in Leesburg. Rumors of Yankees crossing the Potomac are of hourly occurance, and public apprehension has been constantly on the quive [sic].*
> *Business of all kinds has been almost totally suspended, and one hears of nothing and dreams of nothing but the hobgoblins of war.*

But soon even the civilians calmed down, and it was all quiet on the Potomac again. C.H. Nourse, principal of the Loudoun Female Collegiate Institute, was able to announce

124

that his school had re-opened and that the girls there "will be as safe from danger as in any place on the border."

McClellan returned to Washington and wrote to his wife: "How weary I am of all this business! Care after care, blunder after blunder, trick upon trick." But just three days after the battle Colonel Devens assembled the remains of his regiment and addressed them:

> Soldiers of Massachusetts, men of Worcester County, with these fearful gaps in your lines, with the recollection of the terrible struggle of Monday fresh upon your thoughts, with the knowledge of the bereaved and soul-striken ones at home weeping for those they will see no more on earth, with that hospital before your eyes filled with wounded and maimed comrades, I ask you now if you are ready again to meet the traitorous foe who are endeavoring to subvert our government and who are crushing under the iron heel of despotism the liberties of a part of our country? Would you go next week? Would you go tomorrow? Would you go this moment?

To each of these questions the young men responded with a shouted "Yes!"

A Massachusetts woman, an invalid, sent Devens a pair of stockings she had made, asking that he give them "to the bravest man in the battle of Ball's Bluff." Devens awarded them to Captain Chase Philbrick, the man whose timorous reconnaissance and erroneous report had caused the senseless battle to be fought. Said Devens: "I . . . told him to wear them until I found a braver man in the fight. I think they will be worn out before I do."

There were ruffled feathers among some of the officers on both sides after the battle. Colonel Edward Hinks, 19th Massachusetts, who was in command on Harrison's Island, reported that "the remnant of the Tammany Regiment, under the command of Major Bon [probably Major Peter Bowe], deserted its post in the entrenchments on the island at an early hour of the forenoon of the 22nd, and passed to the Maryland shore, in disobedience of orders, while I was engaged in arranging for the removal of the wounded and the burial of the dead." Stone, however, advised Hinks that he himself had ordered the movement of the Tammany Regiment and he indirectly reprimanded him: "Commanding officers are cautioned against making unnecessary and rash statements in their reports, especially in cases where the honor and reputations of other regiments may be involved."

Soldiers were jealous of the reputation of their regiment, and they were fond of comparing their own to others. Lieutenant Holmes told his father: "I think we fought better than the 15th." Sergeant Theodore Compass, also of the 20th Massachusetts, said, "Our boys fought like tigers." Sergeant Compass, a 28-year-old artist from Randolf, Massachusetts, was critical of the Tammany Regiment, and he wrote to his friend Edmund Cuttle back in Randolf: "I have talked to over 200 men, and they all say the Tammany run [sic] back to their boats, before the order came, and they didn't support the advance at all. . . . The three boats they had were filled with wounded, who were crossed over to the island by the Tammany men, as also many cowards of the Tammany crossed with them all the time." Colonel Lee complained of two companies of the California Regiment which "did not move forward with alacrity; they still lay on the ground."

On the Confederate side, Lieutenant Colonel Jenifer's after action report, inaccurate in several respects, caused a brouhaha. He not only claimed to have captured prisoners belonging to the New York Zouaves, the 4th Massachusetts and the 19th Massachusetts—none of which were present on the field—he aroused the ire of the other senior officers by giving the impression that he had been in command of the entire field. Evans called Jenifer on the carpet, and in a supplemental report to Richmond he called attention to the fact that Jenifer had not been aware of the battle plan and had been placed in charge of only the five companies of infantry and the cavalry given him at the start of the battle.

On both sides of the river there were rumors of signals having been made to the enemy. The son of Thomas Swann, ex-mayor of Baltimore, who had a house near Leesburg, was accused of signaling to the Union forces. Francis Buxton of the United States Secret Service reported four days after the battle: "I know from an undoubted source, that signals were made from the Maryland shore when the first boat crossed, which enabled the rascals to be ready for just what they are waiting for, to entrap a small force at a disadvantage." It is most unlikely that signals were made from either side.

In Shanks Evans's native state there were some who felt that the failure of the Loudoun militia to muster and come to the aid of their hero reflected unfavorably on the people of Loudoun County. The Charleston *Courier* thundered that "while Loudoun County may be agriculturally the garden spot of the Commonwealth, politically it is one of the foulest festers upon its surface. . . . You can hardly name a family in certain neighborhoods that has not a fibre of Lincolnism fastened somewhere in the household."

It can be attributed to the ferocity with which both sides fought that each believed the forces of the other to have been immensely superior in numbers to its own. Evans and his men received the thanks of the Confederate Congress for "the brilliant victory achieved by them over largely superior forces of the enemy." Jenifer in his report said "the enemy numbered 4,000", and Evans reported that his force "drove an enemy four times their number from the soil of Virginia."

As for the Federals, Stone reported that his force was outnumbered "nearly, if not quite three to one", and McClellan told his wife that Baker "was outnumbered three to one."

Colonel Lee said flatly that "the loss of the battle is due to the fact that we fought with 1,600 men against 3,200 men." In 1919—fifty-eight years after the battle—Lee's former adjutant, Charles Peirson, was still repeating these figures. Wistar thought there were 5,000-6,000 Confederates on the field.

In fact, the forces engaged on both sides at Ball's Bluff were about equal: each had between 1,600 and 1,700 men on the field. But Southerners continued to believe that Evans had defeated a much larger force, and Northern participants and Northern historians persisted in believing that the Union force had been overwhelmed by superior numbers of the enemy.

The shock of battle affected not only those who fought on the field but spread in ever-widening circles, first to Leesburg and Edwards Ferry, then on to Richmond and Washington, and finally (in spite of a clumsy attempt on the part of Secretary of State William Seward to impose a censorship on all news of the battle) through the telegraph wires to newspapers, and by them to the homes of anxious parents, wives, sweethearts, relatives and friends. Affected too were all who were concerned with their country and its cause—and this was about everybody in the land.

In the South the battle was hailed as a great victory, and it gave a boost to Southern morale; in the North there was consternation, and Henry A. Stewart, a Southern sympathizer in the Union capital, wrote Judah Benjamin, the newly appointed Confederate Secretary of War: "The confusion in Washington is greater than after the battle of Bull Run." Indeed, the shock of the disaster at Ball's Bluff on the North appears to have been greater than that felt after larger disasters later in the war. George Bruce, writing after the war of the reaction in Massachusetts, said that Ball's Bluff "produced a shock in this community scarcely second to any battle of the war." People were singularly unprepared for the defeat. First Bull Run could be explained away, but the rout of Baker's force had been such a clear-cut victory for the South that Northerners were stunned.

Congressman Alfred Ely, ignorant of the bloody battles still to come, predicted that "this battle at Leesburg, when the history of the war is written, will stand forth as one of the severest and most bloody conflicts." No one then suspected that in the history of the war Ball's Bluff would be scarcely more than a footnote. Yet the Boston *Journal* was nearly correct when it said: "Considering the numbers engaged, it is one of the severest actions ever fought on this continent," and Eppa Hunton, who fought in many a more famous battle, was probably right when he wrote long after the war that "for the force engaged on each side, this was the most complete victory of the war."

In the North it was called a "melancholy disaster" a "massacre," "the most atrocious military murder in history." One soldier declared: "There does not seem to be a redeeming feature in the whole business. They went on a fool's errand—went without means, and then persisted in their folly after it became clear." The New York *Tribune* (October 28) concluded: "It seems to have been another of those careless experiments by which, at the caprice of inconsiderate men, the hearts of thousands are torn, and a hundred homes made wretched." But other newspapers agreed with the Springfield (Massachusetts) *Republican*, which thought there was a good deal of glory in the battle: "The facts in regard to General Baker and his command will equal the most daring and gallant exploits ever recorded in ancient or modern times."

A writer for the New York *World* (October 30) found the tale of the battle romantic: "We are all tired of accounts of the petty conflicts which have marked this war. . . . But I say that this conflict, on the Northern side, was most heroically fought and in a true sacrificial spirit. There is nothing like it in our history. . . . Our little band was pent up in a narrow and defenseless slaughter pen. . . . A splendid central picture, which will furnish a theme for American poets and painters long after the feebler tints and groupings of this tumult shall have faded out."

The battle did inspire a few artists and a considerable number of poets or would-be poets. Lincoln's 11-year-old son, "Willie", wrote a poem, "Lines on the Death of Colonel Baker," which he sent to the *National Republican*. "A Southern Lady" wrote a poem entitled "The Battle of Leesburg," dedicated to Colonel Barksdale of the 13th Mississippi. Not many of these rhymes would appeal today, but two became instantly popular and survived in anthologies for many years.

It was reported that the Confederates had said that fewer Massachusetts officers would have been killed if they had not been too proud to surrender. This inspired Brigadier General Frederick W. Lander (who had been in Washington on the day of the battle but whose brigade included the 20th Massachusetts) to write a poem that began:

> Aye, deam us proud, for we are more
> Than proud of all our mighty dead.

The penultimate stanza made famous the names of several junior officers as well as the regiment:

> Pride, 'tis our watchword; "clear the boats,"
> "Holmes, Putnam, Bartlett, Peirson—Here"
> And while this crazy wherry floats,
> "Let's save the wounded," cries Revere

The second poem to win acclaim, "The Vacant Chair" by Henry S. Washburn, brought tears to eyes of many a parent. It was written in memory of 18-year-old Second Lieutenant John William ("Willie") Grout of Company D, 15th Massachusetts, who was struck in the head by a Confederate bullet while trying to swim to Harrison's Island. His body was washed ashore on November 5 and returned to his family. Willie was the only son of Mr. and Mrs. Jonathan Grout of Worcester, Massachusetts, and they gave him a lavish funeral a week later. The Grout's pastor at the Union Congregational Church paid a remarkable tribute to the young man: "Though the child of affluence, privilege, and indulgence, and exposed to the temptations incident to life in a city, he was yet above all reproach or suspicion in respect of his habits and associ-ates." The first and last of Washburn's seven stanzas ended with

> *We shall meet, but we will miss him,*
> *There will be one vacant chair;*
> *We shall linger to caress him*
> *While we breathe our evening prayer.*

The third stanza was particularly touching:

> *At our fireside sad and lonely*
> *Often will the bosom swell,*
> *At remembrance of the story*
> *How our noble Willie fell.*

The poem was set to music, and there are those today who can sing it.

Although not as many chairs were made vacant by Ball's Bluff as by the great battles that followed in the war, to those who lost their young men it mattered not at all whether the battle in which they fell was large or small. Nor was it of any consequence to those left with empty coat sleeves or fitted with wooden legs whether they had left their severed limbs at Shiloh or Ball's Bluff. For the dead, the wounded, and those who love them—a battle is a battle is a battle.

9.
The Wounded and Dead

Casualties are the dead, wounded, and missing, including those who deserted or were taken prisoner. For the military, the concept of casualties is utilitarian: it means simply those who after a battle, for whatever reason, are unable to continue to perform their accustomed duties. Casualty figures include those who can never return to their units and those who eventually will. There are often discrepancies in casualty figures, for much depends upon when the count is made. The total figure is largest immediately after a battle; later some of the missing turn up, some of the wounded return to duty after a few days or a few months, prisoners sometimes escape or are exchanged—the names of all these casualties return to the muster roll. On the other hand, the list of the killed is always smallest immediately after a battle; the dead never return and the mortally wounded die later. It is often difficult to count the total number killed, for some of the wounded (such as many amputees in the Civil War) do not survive their operations; other wounded die weeks later at places distant from their units. Where bodies cannot be found—as was the case with many who were drowned in the Potomac below Ball's Bluff—they can only be carried as missing.

The casualty figures published in the *Official Records* (reproduced here) are certainly inaccurate. They do not tell how many among the missing were, in fact, dead, nor how many

UNION CASUALTIES

	Killed		Wounded		Missing		
	OFFICERS	EM	OFFICERS	EM	OFFICERS	EM	TOTAL
15th Mass	2	12	4	57	8	219	302
20th Mass	2	13	6	38	6	129	194
Tammany Regt.	3	4	—	6	6	114	133
Calif. Regt	3	10	3	37	6	222	281
6th N.Y. Btry.	—	—	1	—	—	—	1
1st R.I. Arty.	—	—	—	5	—	4	9
1st US Arty.	—	—	1	—	—	—	1
TOTAL	10	39	15	143	26	688	921
	49		**158**		**714**		

were captured. Confederate casualty figures are notoriously inaccurate, but for the battle of Ball's Bluff, where the Southern forces were left in undisputed possession of the field after the fight, they are certainly more accurate than the Union numbers. To the list of Confederate dead must be added at least one officer (Colonel Burt) and three privates who died of wounds; it would be safe to assume that the wounds of other Confederates also proved mortal. A guess of 45 killed or mortally wounded would be a likely estimate. There is no way of checking the number of wounded who recovered.

Of the Union casualty figures in the *Official Records*, the number given for those killed (49) is undoubtedly the most inaccurate. A Union burial party interred 47, and the officer in charge estimated that another 20 or 25 were still unburied on the field; at least 18 bodies were found washed up on the banks of the Potomac in or near Washington, and the Confederates found others; probably at least a dozen died of wounds. Evans reported that he sent 529 prisoners south and

CONFEDERATE CASUALTIES

	Killed		Wounded		Missing		
	OFFICERS	EM	OFFICERS	EM	OFFICERS	EM	TOTAL
13th Miss.	1	3	—	2	—	1	7
17th Miss.	2	—	1	8	—	—	11
18th Miss.	—	22	7	56	—	—	85
8th Va.	—	8	4	39	1	—	52
TOTAL	3	33	12	105	1	1	155
	36		**117**		**2**		

that 24 seriously wounded prisoners were kept at Leesburg, at least two of whom died. Possibly there were more wounded, but Evans was unlikely to have underestimated the number of prisoners taken. If we assume Evans's figure is correct, this leaves 161 men listed as missing and unaccounted for on the Union rolls. While at least one and possibly a few more hid and later made their way back to the Union lines, the majority of the missing probably drowned. The total number killed or mortally wounded was most likely just over 200 on the Union side.

If the numbers of those who died in prisons are added, the Union dead as a result of the battle would be significantly higher, though no one has attempted to estimate the number who died at Richmond. Less than two months after the battle, Captain Clark Simonds wrote of five men of the 15th Massachusetts who had died in prison. Not all of these died of wounds; many died of diseases and were buried in unmarked graves.

The casualty figures in the *Official Records* for the various units are not reconcilable in detail with those given by the officers who were in the best position to know. According to the *Official Records*, for example, the casualties for the California Regiment were 12 officers and 269 enlisted men, but Lieutenant Colonel Wistar in his report of November 7 (not given in the *Official Records*, but reproduced in Wistar's autobiography) stated that 16 out of 18 officers and 305 out of 570 enlisted men were casualties. *

The Union wounded who were not fortunate enough to be ferried over to Harrison's Island were left on the ground to be collected by the Confederates along with their own wounded. The Confederate treatment of the wounded, their own as well as their enemy's, was careless, not to say callous. Except for their guesses as to casualties, the after action reports of the Confederate officers, with the exception of one, made no mention of the wounded. Colonel Featherston said that at 11:00 P.M.—some four hours after the battle ended—he sent out ninety men to collect the dead and wounded. There were regimental surgeons but no field hospitals. The wounded were simply distributed among the houses in Leesburg and the surrounding farms. Surgeon Revere of the 20th Massachusetts was the only doctor actually on the battlefield. After his capture, he was not permitted to assist the wounded but was kept with the other officers taken prisoner. Some fathers of the 8th Virginia boys searched for and found their wounded sons on the field and carried them home.

The Union handling of their wounded was somewhat better, but certainly inadequate. Lieutenant Colonel Wistar, one of the last of the wounded to be rowed to Harrison's Island, was stuffed into the metallic boat, his feet dragging in the water. An Irishman, wounded in both legs, held him in place, hugging him tightly with both arms. "No fear for ye, Cornel," he said. "I'll hold ye fast or we'll both go over together jist."

On the island Wistar was taken to the farm and put in an enclosure filled with other wounded ranged around the yard,

---

*Historians have a wide range of numbers to choose from. Baltz listed total casualties as 313; Fatout gave the number as 331. Wistar's figure of 321 is probably as near correct as any.

heads to the fence. Later he wrote: "I was insensible and fainting, and supposed I was to die in the course of the night." To add to the misery of the wounded, it began to rain.

There were two surgeons on the island: Samuel Haven, Jr., thirty, of Worcester, assistant surgeon of the 15th Massachusetts, and Nathan Hayward, thirty-one, of Roxbury, assistant surgeon of the 20th Massachusetts. They did what they could. Haven found two inches of candle stuck in a bottle and by its light he amputated Lieutenant Colonel Ward's leg. (Ward, thirty-five years old, survived his operation and recovered in time to be killed at Gettysburg).

Among the wounded was Private Samuel Sibley of Company H, 15th Massachusetts. Older than most, the 40-year-old miller from Sutton had been shot through both thighs early in the morning but had continued firing until a third bullet shattered his knee. Chaplain Scandlin stood by while a surgeon removed the bullets from his thighs, and Sibley asked, "Chaplain, will you find my wallet and put those bullets in? I'll want them sometime." Scandlin put the bullets away and a few days later recorded that "from that time throughout he has been bright, cheerful and hopeful." But Private Sibley died of his wounds two weeks after the battle.

Over on the Maryland shore were the senior surgeons of the Massachusetts regiments: Dr. Joseph Bates, fifty, of the 15th, had been sick in bed for weeks, but he got up to attend to the wounded, and Dr. Henry Bryant, forty-one, of the 20th, was on hand to load the wounded into canal boats to be sent down to Edwards Ferry. But the young assistant surgeons on Harrison's Island had difficulty getting their patients carried across the island, into the boats and over to the Maryland shore. Dr. Hayward in a long, bitter letter to his father (November 3) painted an ugly picture of the scene on Harrison's:

> Our greatest difficulty was to induce men to carry
> the wounded to the river. The Tammany men be-

*haved disgracefully. . . . The musicians of the 15th
Mass. Regt. also showed the white feather, refused
duty and ran away. . . . It was thought the Secessionists might shell the Island at daybreak, and it
was therefore desirable to remove all the wounded
to the Maryland shore before morning. By tearing
down all the doors in . . . two houses we succeeded in getting litters enough to take every
wounded man down to the shore. . . . All those
employed in the early part of the evening to move
the litters took the opportunity of crossing themselves, and did not return. No order or discipline
existed in the boats; they were filled with the
strongest and most impudent, and started leaving
the poor wounded behind. When I reached the
shore there lay 16 poor wounded fellows, including
three of our own officers, who had been lying,
some of them, two hours in a drizzling rain. We
succeeded in getting a boat and putting all our 16
into it, having laid straw in the bottom of the boat,
which was wet and muddy. . . . It was necessary to
show my revolver to keep off intruders. . . . And
many a man on our side, that day, was threatened
by his officers and in some instances struck with the
sword. We reached the Maryland side without difficulty, pulling the scow by a rope which had been
stretched across by Colonel Hinks' men. . . . When
we reached the shore . . . we could get none of the
lazy Pennsylvanians, who occupied the bank, to lift
a hand to help us, in spite of objurations. . . . We
got them at length into a canal boat which lay in
readiness with Dr. Bryant on board.*

Once the wounded reached the canal boats their lot improved somewhat, for the ride to Edwards Ferry was smooth.
So restful was it after the fury of battle and the trauma of
wounds that at least one man fell asleep. At Edwards Ferry

the wounded were hurriedly separated from the dead, who were carried to the porch of an old store and laid in a row. A soldier there, curious to see if he knew any, lifted the rubber sheet from the face of one and was astonished to see him blink his eyes and look around.

From Edwards Ferry the wounded were transported to their regiments to be cared for by their own regimental surgeons. There was, in fact, almost no other place for them, for the Union army had made inadequate provision for sick and wounded soldiers. Clement Alexander Finley, the 64-year-old Surgeon General and the Union army's chief medical officer, was a distinguished-looking gentleman of the old school—in his youth he had been considered the handsomest man in the army—but he had not the foggiest notion of what was required of him. Frederick Law Olmsted, Secretary of the Sanitary Commission, characterized him as "a self-satisfied, supercilious, bigoted blockhead." When the war started, Finley was asked what additional medical personnel he thought would be required for the bloody struggle ahead. He replied that he thought forty more medical officers and fifty "medical cadets" would be sufficient. Consequently, regiments were forced to care for their own as best they could in makeshift field hospitals and private homes.

Although the facilities were woefully inadequate, the men were at least cared for by doctors and orderlies they knew and who knew them; they received personal attention. They also received visits from home. After Ball's Bluff Governor Andrew sent from Boston William Lee as his personal representative along with a doctor. They were followed shortly by friends and relatives bearing delicacies and welcome letters from home. Chaplain Scandlin noted in his diary: "The interest and sympathy of Massachusetts is met on every hand. There are delegates from every town connected with our regiment; so many callers that they fairly trouble us."

Lieutenant Richard Derby also commented on the crowds

of people who came not only from Massachusetts but from Washington: "Nobody blamed them for their anxiety, although they were really in the way." The town of Fitchburg began a custom, continued throughout the war, of sending a committee to the front after every battle in which its own Company B, 15th Massachusetts, participated. Four Fitchburg men, one a doctor, journeyed to Poolesville. They stayed several days and carried back with them two of their wounded.

One of the women who came out from Washington to Poolesville to nurse the wounded described her experiences:

> *After I had tucked a fine little fellow of eighteen into his bed for the night, and had made the pillow easy for the stump of his arm, and had his thanks for the comfort, I spoke to him tenderly of his loss, and the manly answer was: "I do not regret it; it was lost in a good cause, and I do not wish it otherwise."*

The feeling was general and was sustained throughout the war that the loss of limbs and life was a cost that had to be bourne and that the cause was worth the loss. Although the Revere brothers survived Ball's Bluff unscathed, later in the war they were both killed—Major Paul Revere at Gettysburg and Surgeon Edward Revere at Antietam. A family friend (P. Sprague), who had himself lost a son in the war, wrote to their father, Joseph Warren Revere: "Both your noble sons fell on the field of successful battle, in a righteous cause—a cause of justice, freedom and humanity, and all the blessings of good government." Lieutenant James Jackson Lowell, twenty-four, who had been first scholar in his class when he was graduated from Harvard, left law school to accept a commission in the 20th Massachusetts. When he died of wounds four days after the battle of Ball's Bluff, a friend wrote to his mother: "Don't you think Jim's dying has accomplished as much as his life may have done?"

Lowell's cousin, the golden-haired William Lowell Putnam, twenty-one, was another promising young man whose life was snuffed out. Lieutenant Henry Sturgis had carried him off the battlefield on his back and then saw him carried over to Harrison's Island, but he had a bullet in his bowels and died the next day. Young Putnam had possessed most of life's gifts: he was tall, exceptionally handsome ("the handsomest man at Harvard College") and intelligent; he was born into a socially and culturally prominent family of considerable wealth; he had a charming personality and was ever popular; at Harvard he had received the best education the country could offer. He dreamed of becoming an historian. His mother felt that he died in a great and just cause, but she added: "And yet how many and what hopes passed with that passing breath, those that his young heart had cherished . . . . those which admiring comrades had set in him . . . . those that hearts already bereaved had treasured for him." In dying he gave up, she said, "projects of great and noble accomplishment."

When the wounded were able to be moved in safety they were allowed to return home to convalesce. Wistar lay for nine weeks without being able to turn his head because of the wound in his jaw. His right arm required a second operation; it was saved, but remained forever paralyzed. (A second wound at Antietam left his remaining arm partially paralyzed.) He was eventually sent home to Philadelphia, arriving at his father's house in time for Christmas.

The bullet that struck Oliver Wendell Holmes, Jr., passed from side to side through his chest, narrowly missing his heart and lungs. Two weeks after the battle he started home. His father met him in Philadelphia and found him pale and barely able to walk, but in good spirits. Dr. Holmes engaged six seats on the train to Boston and spread a mattress across them. For the first but not the last time, he carried his wounded son home to Charles Street. There he was put into his sister's room and lavished with all the attention a loving family could give.

At first young Holmes was reluctant to speak of the battle, but audiences of admiring young women soon loosened his tongue. Dr. Holmes wrote to his friend John Motley in Vienna:

> *Wendell is a great pet in his character of young hero with wounds in the heart. He receives visits en grand seigneur. I envy my white Othello with a semicircle of young Desdemonas about him listening to the often told story which they will have over again.*

Mrs. Holmes kept a list of "Visitors to the Wounded Lieutenant." It included Professor Louis Agassiz's daughter, Ida; president Cornelius Conway Felton of Harvard; Charles Sumner, senior senator from Massachusetts; novelist Anthony Trollope, who in November was visiting Boston; and Fanny Dixwell, the young officer's future wife, who came accompanied by her mother. In late March 1862, Lieutenant Holmes was well enough to return to his regiment.

Holmes had very narrowly escaped death. Other seriously wounded men were not so fortunate and day after day they died. Private Albert Stackpole of the 20th Massachusetts died three days after the fight; he was an 18-year-old boy from Nantucket. Some lingered for only a few days, some for weeks. It was the same across the river in Virginia. Flavius ("Stormer") Osburn of Snickersville, (today Bluemont) Virginia, eldest of four sons, died the day after the battle. Colonel Burt of the 15th Mississippi died on October 26. Private Samuel Flippin, a 22-year-old farmer from Holly Springs, Mississippi, whose leg was amputated, lingered on until November 29.

Ai Osborne, a 28-year-old millwright from Fitchburg, Massachusetts, and Thomas Taylor, a 28-year-old sailor, both of the 15th Massachusetts, were wounded and left on the field. Eventually they were brought into Leesburg. As Osborne was about to be taken from the ambulance, he said, "Take Taylor out first. He is wounded worse than I am," but this proved not to be the case. When Osborne's leg was amputated close to his body, Taylor was well enough to commiserate with him. "Yes," said Osborne, "I know you are very sorry, Tom, but what will poor mother say?" He died on December 1.

On the day after the battle, Colonel Hinks sent Lieutenant James G.G. Dodge across the river under a flag of truce to ask permission for Union surgeons to care for the wounded still on the ground. Lieutenant Dodge, twenty-one years old, stood only five feet, three inches high. He had lost his overcoat, so he threw a blanket over his shoulders when he crossed to the Virginia shore. On the bank of the river at the foot of the bluff he encountered the detritus of the Union force: tins of cartridges, broken muskets, bits of uniforms and equipment, and two wounded men calling for water. A Confederate soldier led him to the top of the bluff and helped him search for an officer. Dodge noted a number of civilians on the field joking and laughing with Confederate soldiers.

Dodge identified himself to an officer who rode up on his horse. "Where are your credentials?" the officer asked.

Dodge drew himself up. "I have none," he said. "In our army the *word* of an officer is sufficient."

"How in hell do I know you're an officer?"

Little Lieutenant Dodge leaped up on a stone, jerked the blanket from his shoulders, and, pointing to the bars on his shoulder straps, said: "These are my credentials."

This established, Dodge stated his errand. While the Union request was being debated, Dodge talked with Lieutenant Colonel Jenifer, who asked about his former West Point classmate, General Stone.

The Confederates refused to agree to Union doctors crossing

to assist the wounded unless they consented to remain as Confederate prisoners. Dodge returned with this message to Maryland.

Colonel Hinks, who was conducting the negotiations, found the Confederate terms for sending over doctors unacceptable. However, he sent Captain Thomas Vaughn of the Rhode Island artillery back across the river with another flag of truce to request permission for a burial party to be sent.

Lieutenant Colonel John McGuirk of the 17th Mississippi gave permission for a Union burial party to cross with the stipulation that "no movement of troops should be made from the island to the Maryland shore while the burial party was employed." McGuirk later explained: "I did this from the fact that there was a large force on the island, which I could hold in check with my small force and prevent the troops from re-enforcing the enemy who had landed at Edwards Ferry." Hinks agreed to McGuirk's terms, and Captain Vaughn was sent over again with a ten-man burial detail and Chaplain Christopher Cushing of North Brookfield, Massachusetts. While the Union burial party worked, McGuirk kept a sharp eye on the river. When he saw two boats leaving the island he threatened to keep Vaughn a prisoner unless the boats returned.

Lieutenant Colonel Jenifer also reported a violation of the truce. Some of his cavalry pickets were fired on several times by soldiers on Harrison's Island and he was indignant: "This disgraceful act was committed by some of the troops under the command of Colonel Hinks, of the Federal army, who was perfectly aware that some of his officers and men were on the Virginia side burying their dead."

Vaughn found most of the bodies in the woods around the open field at the top of the bluff. All the caps and shoes of the dead had been taken; in some instances jackets were missing; buttons had been torn off, and in two cases all the clothing had been removed except the shirts. The pockets of the dead had been thoroughly rifled. So much had been removed that, according to Chaplain Cushing, there were only three instances in which anything could be found that would identify the bodies: "Stitched to the trousers of one was found the name of Captain Henry H. Alden, Company H, Tammany Regiment; under the body of another was an envelope superscribed James Douglas; into the top of the socks of another were beautifully inwrought the letters W.H.H.L."

Vaughn and his party found and buried forty-seven bodies, which he estimated was about two-thirds of the dead on the field. Only two Confederate dead were found. They came upon two severely wounded Union soldiers, but these had to be turned over to the Confederates, who carried them to Leesburg. Chaplain Cushing described for the Worcester *Spy* how the dead were buried:

> *Our dead were buried with their clothes on, laying the body upon the side in trenches, usually two, three or four, side by side, never one upon another, and in the same trench there was in only one instance so many as eleven. The faces were covered with leaves, and then the body was covered with earth to the depth of from three to five feet, and a stone was placed at the head and foot of each grave.*

Chaplain Cushing mercifully refrained from descriptions of the young bodies. Burying such human remains is sickening work. When at last it was done and Vaughn returned to Harrison's Island, he put his arms around the neck of his friend, Lieutenant John Reynolds, and exclaimed over and over again, "Horrible! Horrible! Horrible!"

Somewhere on the field, eventually found, but not it seems by Captain Vaughn and his detail, was the body of Private James Allen, a 22-year-old shoemaker from Northampton, Massachusetts. He had enlisted in the 15th Massachusetts on

May 25, 1861, was mustered into the federal service on July 12, and was killed scarcely more than three months later. His body today is still on the field, his grave there is the only one whose occupant is known.

On March 12, 1862, when Loudoun County was in Federal hands, the New York *Times* reported that "a detachment of the 1st Michigan Cavalry rode to Ball's Bluff . . . . and buried the whitened bones of the brave Union soldiers who fell in that field on October last." Perhaps not even then were all the remains decently buried, for Colonel James M. More, who inspected the field after the war, said in his report (dated December 8, 1865):

> No kindly feeling seems to have actuated those living in the vicinity to care for the dead, and after they were permitted to lie for days, exposed to the ravages of animals, were only covered with earth when the air became foetid with the odor from the bodies.

On October 30, 1861, when Stone asked Evans if he could send supplies to the wounded prisoners of war, he also asked if the body of Captain Alden could be brought back. Permission was granted, and on November 6 a party crossed the Potomac, dug up Alden's corpse and brought it back; it was sent to his family in Massachusetts for burial.

In the days that followed the battle, bodies of the drowned were found floating down the river or washed up on the shores downstream. On November 3 the Baltimore *Sun* reported five bodies taken out of the river near Chain Bridge: "They were so much mutilated as to be beyond recognition. Only one of them was apparently wounded." On the following day thirteen more bodies were drawn from the river. One corpse, nearly naked, was found washed against the wharf at the foot of 6th Street in Washington; another was found amid a pile of drift-

This illustration depicts a patrol pulling bodies of Union dead from the Potomac near Great Falls. Other bodies washed up at Georgetown and Washington and as far away as Fort Washington, more than fifty miles downstream from Ball's Bluff. Many of the missing were never found.

wood near Long Bridge; still others at Georgetown. Further downstream, opposite Fort Washington, a soldier was found with a round mirror, a Bible and a lock of hair in his pocket.

The corpses of those slain and buried on the field have not been allowed to rest in peace. Unless there are today some unknown graves in the woods that now cover most of the battlefield (and this is possible) all of the bodies have been buried at least twice, and just in the past thirty years there have been several attempts by federal authorities to dig up and transplant the bones of the twenty-five now buried in a circle around a flag pole in the smallest national cemetery. Even Baker, whose corpse was one of the few carried back during the battle, has been buried three times.

From Poolesville, where Captain Young had taken Baker's body, the corpse was taken to Washington, where it was embalmed, clothed in a clean uniform and put on display at the home of James Wilson Webb at the corner of 14th and F Streets. Webb was a former newspaper proprietor and was soon to be United States minister to Brazil. Lincoln had wanted the body placed in the East room at the White House, but Mrs. Lincoln was redecorating and she thought the White House was not in suitable condition for such a purpose. The flag-draped coffin, covered with white flowers and evergreens, was carried out of the Webb home by six colonels; a large military contingent escorted the hearse to the Congressional Cemetery. The hearse was followed by president Lincoln, Vice president Hannibal Hamlin, members of the cabinet, the chief and associate justices of the Supreme Court, and numerous congressmen.

There was criticism of the military escort. "No Cossack or Bashi Bazouk," wrote the reporter for the New York *Tribune*, "was ever half so rude, raw, undisciplined and uncivilized in appearance as this cavalry selected for a purpose of ceremony." The infantry, too, was unsatisfactory, the *Tribune* reported. Some carried their muskets like fishing poles, lounged on one leg, scratched themselves, talked in loud voices and otherwise were unmilitary and irreverent.

After suitable eulogies and burial in Washington, Baker's body was exhumed and sent to San Francisco, with stops along the way at Philadelphia (where the corpse was laid out in Independence Hall) and New York. There was another funeral in San Francisco on December 11. Services were held in the Music Hall where, according to the San Francisco *Daily Evening Bulletin*, there was such "squeezing, jamming and crowding as probably never was witnessed before in San Francisco." Then the body was interred at Lone Mountain Cemetery. Citizens of Oregon were unsuccessful in efforts to have the body transferred there.

Not long after World War II, president Truman and General George C. Marshall were walking over the Ball's Bluff battlefield, and Truman, seeing the stone erected by unknown hands that marks the spot where Baker is supposed to have fallen, wondered where Baker's body was buried. Marshall did not know, so when Truman went back to Washington he asked Senator Wayne Morse of Oregon. Morse investigated and told Truman that Baker was buried in a private cemetery in San Francisco. But Morse's investigation had been superficial and Truman was misinformed. Only a few years earlier it had been decided that Lone Mountain Cemetery stood in the way of development and it had been destroyed. On May 21, 1940, Baker's bones and those of his wife, who had died ten years after her husband, were dug up and thrown together into a single grave at the San Francisco Presidio. A simple headstone marks the spot. As the army is abandoning the Presidio as a military post, Baker's bones may be moved to a fourth grave.

10.
The Prisoners

The Confederates captured more than 550 Union soldiers at Ball's Bluff; the Federals captured just one Confederate: First Lieutenant J. Owen Berry of Company G, 8th Virginia, who was taken prisoner when he inadvertently rode into the lines of the California Regiment. Six soldiers hustled him down the bluff to the boats. As he was about to embark with some Union wounded, a captain asked who he was and when told he was a prisoner of war growled, "Hang him!" Shocked, someone repeated that he was a prisoner, but the captain was unmoved, "Hang him!" he said again. Fortunately, as Berry later told General Beauregard, "this appeal was not seconded by any voice that I heard."

Berry was safely conveyed to Harrison's Island and from there to the Maryland shore, where he was placed under guard at the camp of the California Regiment, about two miles back from the river on the road to Poolesville. There, he said, "at daylight on the following Tuesday morning the men of the brigade in large numbers assembled around my tent and for three hours abused me with the vilest imprecations." In the afternoon his arms were pinioned at the elbows, in spite of his loud protests, and he was taken to Lieutenant Colonel Wistar. Suffering dreadfully from his three wounds, Wistar can be forgiven for not thinking as clearly as usual. He offered to release Berry if he would promise not to escape before he was turned over to division headquarters. Berry reluctantly agreed and the "slight ligature" (as Wistar described the rope) was untied. He was then taken to the camp of the 15th Massachusetts just outside Poolesville.

"The next morning," said Berry, "for a few hours I was insulted by both officers and men." After breakfast he was taken to General Stone, to whom Berry indignantly protested his treatment, reciting a list of abuses to which he had been subjected. Stone apologized and "expressed regret" for the conduct of his troops. The following Monday, October 28, Lieutenant Church Howe took the prisoner to Washington, and he was placed in the Old Capitol Building, then used as a prison. A week later, he fashioned a rope out of blanket strips and escaped to Virginia, perhaps aided by his father, a former clerk in the Census Bureau who still lived in Georgetown.

After Berry told the story of his treatment to General Pierre Beauregard, the Confederates lodged a formal complaint. Stone went to see Wistar and pointed out that Berry's rights as a prisoner of war had been violated when Wistar demanded his parole as the price of freeing his arms. Wistar later said: "I was, of course, properly mortified and self-rebuked at the just construction thus placed on the condition I had thoughtlessly imposed, but Stone said he had already explained the circumstances and offered verbal reparations on my behalf."

The Hague Convention on Land Warfare and the Geneva Convention which laid down rules governing the relations between prisoners of war and their captors are twentieth-century creations, but in the nineteenth century officers who were gentlemen strove to conduct themselves as such—at least in the early stages of this war. However, punctilious behavior to prisoners was soon to yield to political considerations.

In the handling of prisoners, the conduct of the Confederate soldiers on the field was unexceptionable. Lieutenant Colonel McGuirk lent his horse to Colonel Cogswell, who was wounded in the hand; some of the prisoners were given bread that was being brought up for the Confederates; none of the Union soldiers complained of ill treatment. Private Henry Greenwood, a 25-year-old printer in the 15th Massachusetts, was among those captured after dark by Berkeley and White at the foot of the bluff:

> *After they had demanded our arms . . . they marched us up the hill to go to Leesburg. On the top of the hill, on the field of battle, we could see our dead, who lay as they had fallen or where they had been laid by their comrades. As we passed by the place where we had made our stand in the morning, we could see the enemy's dead. We were taken, as it seemed to me, by a roundabout way to the town.*

In Leesburg the prisoners, at least the enlisted men, were put into the yard around the Loudoun County courthouse, and a large crowd of townspeople, "made frantic by the victory," (as one Union soldier put it) greeted them with cries of "We've got 'em this time!" "Oh you infernal Yankees!" "Make way, Jim, I want to see a yank!"

In a tavern across the street, Colonel Evans, a bottle of peach brandy by his side, prepared to celebrate his victory. A remarkable man was "Shanks" Evans. No one ever spoke of him without mentioning his drinking, but no one appears to have seen him incapacitated or unable to function because of liquor—at least no one could ever prove it. Although later in the war he was court-martialed for being drunk on duty, he was found not guilty. His handling of his brigade at Ball's Bluff, his measured risks and his correct estimates of his enemy's dispositions and intentions—all displayed brilliant generalship.

Eppa Hunton criticized Evans for not appearing on the battlefield, but Evans actually deserves praise rather than censor for resisting the temptation (to which so many nineteenth-century generals succumbed) to rush out and forget his responsibilities in the smoke and excitement of battle. He had no need to prove his bravery: he had done this in the Indian wars and, most recently, at Bull Run. In this battle, with the presence of Gorman's brigade on the Virginia shore at Edwards Ferry and the uncertainty of the movements and intentions of McCall, Evans had positioned himself exactly where he ought to have been, and he had moved his men like a chess master. Shanks Evans may not have conformed to the Southern ideal of a courtly gentleman, but he was a tough, smart soldier.

The captured Union officers were taken to the tavern where Evans genially offered them some of his peach brandy. Cogswell and Evans knew each other well, for they had been at West Point together, Evans being in the class just ahead of Cogswell. After some good-natured banter, Evans produced a parole paper which he asked the Union officers to sign. There is conflicting testimony regarding the exact nature of the parole. An officer in the 20th Massachusetts said later that they were asked to "all agree not to serve again during the war," but this seems unlikely. First Lieutenant J. Evarts Greene of the 15th Massachusetts said that they were merely asked "to sign a parole in which they engaged to report themselves at Richmond within a few days." Greene, a 26-year-old lawyer from North Brookfield, probably paid closer attention to the terms than the others. In any case, none signed.

Cogswell protested, "Shanks, you ought not to offer this to gentlemen." Others chimed in. "You are no gentleman to offer this," one said. Evans flared up angrily, but the affronted Cogswell held his ground. Greene said that "for a few moments a violent collision seemed imminent, but friends of each intervened and some measure of decorum was restored." Evans was so angry that after the Union officers left he ordered

Hunton to have their hands tied, but Hunton, shocked by the order, refused.

It is difficult for us today, accustomed as we are to the barbarous treatment so often imposed on prisoners of modern wars, knowing as well the treatment to which prisoners were subjected later in this same civil war, to understand the indignant response of the Union officers to what appears to have been a generous offer. Hunton thought they refused because they expected to be speedily rescued by the Union army. This would explain their refusal, but not their indignation. No cartel regarding the exchange of prisoners had been negotiated as yet, and it is impossible to imagine, since none of the captured Union officers ever said, exactly what they expected Evans to do for them. Short of setting them free, there was little else he could have done.

Perhaps Evans feared that some attempt would be made to free his prisoners; they were, after all, close to the border and many might be tempted to escape; reason enough to move them as soon as possible further south. So about midnight more than half of the prisoners, officers and enlisted men, were put on the road to Manassas. It rained heavily and most were on foot, though a lumber wagon was provided for those unable to walk. It was a hard march. Some were without coats; many, who had not slept for more than thirty-six hours and had fought all day, were close to exhaustion. They were guarded by a detachment of cavalry and a company of infantry under the command of Captain Otto R. Singleton of the 18th Mississippi. Singleton had been a congressman before the war and later he was to serve in the Confederate congress; the prisoners agreed that he performed his task of moving them twenty-five miles to Manassas "with perfect courtesy and kindness."

Daylight found the weary column still marching. They attracted considerable attention along the way; women ran from their houses to jeer at them, and some shouted, "Kill the damned Yankees!" When at last they reached the Confederate lines near Manassas, they were allowed to rest in and around the Stone House.* Here they were given some corn bread and raw pork, which they cooked themselves over fires made from lathes torn from the building. They were ravenously hungry. Many later declared that this was the best meal they ever ate.

Among those prisoners who remained in Leesburg was Private John H. Richard, Company B, 15th Massachusetts. He had been temporarily blinded by a bullet wound and was led from the battlefield into Leesburg, where he was given a supper of meat, bread, butter and coffee and was well cared for. The next day, however, he and all other prisoners able to travel were marched off toward Manassas. It was an easier march than it had been for their comrades who preceded them, the trip taking two days; they were also issued corn bread and bacon before they left. At Manassas they were not put with the other Ball's Bluff prisoners but in a kind of stockade that housed "the turbulent and rebellious ones of their own forces." There were sheds in the enclosure, but the Confederate prisoners refused to allow the Union prisoners inside, forcing them to sleep in the mud.

The second group of prisoners was sent to Richmond before the first. Private Prichard told of the trip in a train made up of mixed passenger and cattle cars:

> At every station were crowds . . . full of curiosity. . . . Most of them were civil . . . others jeered at, hooted, and taunted us with our misfortunes. . . . "What did you come down here for?" "Come down to steal our niggers, ravish our wives and daughters, and burn our houses, didn't ye?"

*Still standing, this building was the most conspicuous landmark on the battlefield during both of the Bull Run battles.

"Think ye can whip us, hey?" "Didn't do it, did ye, hey?"

In Richmond, said Prichard, the people were "very abusive and scandalous in the abuse and epithets applied to the d—d yankees."

The other, larger, group of prisoners was kept at Manassas for a week and then sent to Richmond in freight cars. Their train, carrying 475 prisoners under escort of Lieutenant Colonel T.C. Johnson of the 19th Georgia, arrived in Richmond at 10:30 on the morning of October 29 and was met by a huge crowd of men, women and children. Confederate guards kept the crowd away from the cars, but the prisoners inside could hear the people shouting as they struggled to catch sight of them: "There's one! See! There's a Yank!" and "Send fifty of them to my plantation and I'll teach them how to pick cotton!" One woman was heard to cry out: "Why don't you send them down the river and make breastworks of them!"

Confederate soldiers lined the streets and made a path for the prisoners. The sidewalks, balconies and house tops were crowded with curious spectators as they were marched down Broad Street on their way to Robert Mayo's tobacco factory at the corner of 25th Street and Cary Street to continued jeers and taunts.

According to the Richmond *Examiner* (October 29), not all the taunts were by Southerners:

> *A portion of the prisoners displayed considerable impudence. One fellow said their turn would come by-and-by, and that Lincoln and Scott would both be in Richmond before a great while. Another remarked to a bystander that they had to hunt for the Confederate soldiers to make them fight, and the bystander reckoned that they fought pretty well when they were found.*

One of the most interesting aspects of this account by the Richmond *Examiner* was the mention of a "negro soldier" in the ranks of the 20th Massachusetts. This was Lewis A. Bell, a free man from Washington, D.C. The presence of Bell on the battlefield and his participation in the fight is corroborated by one other source, which says: "Lewis, a servant of Colonel Cogswell, in the confusion, supplied himself with arms, and loaded and fired with great spirit, until captured with Lieutenant Green."* He was taken to Richmond and treated as a prisoner of war.

It would appear, therefore, that Lewis A. Bell was the first known and positively identified black to take part in a Civil War battle. It was not until a year later (October 28, 1862, at Island Mounds, Missouri) that a black military unit, the 79th U.S. Colored Infantry, fought in a battle. Bell's presence among the prisoners caused a stir in Richmond, and it was noted that he was uneasy. Well he might be, for his status was uncertain. Some men in the crowd muttered that they thought they had seen him before and that he was "what the Yankees term a 'contraband'." Later, in April 1863, the Confederates decreed that "negroes captured will not be regarded as prisoners of war." The fate of Bell is unknown.

Charles Peirson, adjutant of the 20th Massachusetts, described the prison to which he and others were taken:

> *The tobacco warehouse which we occupied is on the main street of Richmond. It was similar to several other buildings and they are all used as Military Prisons, and all called Libby Prison. It is a large three-stored building. . . . The first floor was allotted to the officers captured, some 70 in number, and the other stories filled with men, perhaps 250*

---

*This would be either Jeremiah Green or perhaps J. Evarts Greene, both of the 15th Massachusetts.

of them. In the center of the lower or officers floor is placed the heavy machinery for processing the tobacco, thus dividing the space into two equal sections, and occupying one-half of the floor space, which was 65 x 45 feet.

The windows on the street floors are well protected by iron bars, while those opposite are unprovided with bars, and open upon the yard, but guarded by sentinels stationed there with orders to shoot any prisoners in either story who lean out of the windows. Seven men were shot by these guardsmen while I was confined there. The dying from the nearby hospital were taken to this yard for shipment elsewhere in wagons.

Looking out the barred windows into the street, the prisoners could watch the passersby and frequently saw president Jefferson Davis, to whom they called out derisive remarks. To the tune of "John Brown's Body" they sang, "We'll hang Jeff Davis to a sour apple tree." Lieutenant Isaac Hart of the 20th Indiana composed new lyrics for the popular "Bring Back My Bonny", and in more pensive moments they serenaded him with "Roll on, sweet moments, roll on, and let the poor prisoners go home, go home."

The citizens of Richmond were curious about the Union prisoners. * Alfred Ely, the congressman from Rochester, New York, who had been captured at Bull Run carrying a pistol, **

---

*According to the census of 1860, Richmond had a population of 38,000 and boasted of three incorporated banks, seventeen periodicals and thirty churches.

**Ely was not the only civilian among the prisoners of war. Calvin Huson, Jr., a former district attorney in Rochester, New York, and once an opponent of Ely for Congress, was also a prisoner. He too had been captured at Bull Run. He died of typhoid fever in Richmond.

noted that "our outside doors and sidewalks are so constantly crowded with visitors that it is with difficulty the guard can keep them at a distance." Later he wrote in his diary: "The street has been filled with fashionable carriages, stopping in front of our quarters; and the occupants appear to be genteel people; at the same time, such visits for *mere curiosity*, especially for ladies, do not prove either delicacy or refinement."

Ely was housed with the officers and was himself the object of special curiosity. He wrote: "A Yankee Congressman, how attractive! Barring the music, this cage of American citizens reminds me of Barnum's Museum." Many people of influence obtained permission to enter the prison and talk with the prisoners—so many, in fact, that Ely finally asked the prison commandant "to discriminate and curtail passes to the prison."

In spite of the stream of visitors, boredom was the prisoners' great enemy. They read the newspapers and debated the progress of the war; they played cards, wrote letters, and read the few available books. Some of the officers formed a club, The Richmond Prison Association, "for mutual improvement and amusement." In their meetings, members made speeches, sang songs, recited poems and told stories. Sometimes Confederate officers attended as invited guests. A Sanitary Committee formed by the Association laid down rules governing matters of health and cleanliness. Congressman Ely thought the Association had an effect upon "the decency, good order, and the decorum so essential in a place like this."

Every Sunday and Wednesday the Association organized religious meetings. Many of the prisoners were deeply religious. Ely thought he saw the hand of God in his own predicament. He remembered that his wife had warned him that "work or amusement indulged in upon the Sabbath must, sooner or later, result in disaster." Whether he considered his Sunday jaunt to the Battle of Bull Run as work or amusement he did not say, but he acknowledged its sinfulness: "An all-wide Providence punishes me for a violation of his commandment, a sequence as direct as it is just."

Not every officer was as high minded as the members of the Association. Charles Peirson, who was something of a prude, complained in his diary that "very many of our associates are men of vulgar tastes and habits, so that their society is anything but agreeable. Noise and confusion reign most of the time with a constant jarring of one's sensibilities."

One day Peirson had a visit from a Confederate army surgeon who had received a letter from a mutual friend in Boston asking him to do what he could for Peirson and the other Massachusetts prisoners. He offered to do anything that was in his power, but Peirson, a proud young man, wrote in his diary: "There were many things he might have offered to do, but which I would not ask for."

On one of the upper floors of the tobacco factory Sergeant Luther Goddard, a 34-year-old merchant who had enlisted in the 15th Massachusetts, was put in charge of the 223 men who were housed there. No beds were provided and few possessed blankets; shoes served as pillows. The Confederates supplied food for only two meals a day. ("Worms in the rice, and beef whose 'offense was rank and smelt to Heaven,' were among the common incidents of our living," complained Private Prichard.) Sergeant Goddard organized his men and managed to keep his floor as clean and comfortable as possible. His efforts earned praise for his regiment from his jailors: Under the heading of *The Best of a Bad Lot* the Richmond *Examiner* reported that the "prison authorities give credit to the Yankee prisoners of the Fifteenth Massachusetts Regiment of being the most cleanly, decent and orderly of all brought here."

On November 20 a letter—the first news from the prisoners—arrived at Fitchburg, the home town of Company B, 15th Massachusetts. It was from the company commander, Captain Clark Simonds (he who had stabbed himself in the head with his own sword while marching to the battle). Simonds described the conditions under which he and the others were living and their lack of necessities. His letter was read at a public meeting, and $700 in cash and $100 worth of clothing were immediately offered for the relief of the prisoners. In early December a large box of blankets and clothes arrived in Richmond. Fitchburg's example was followed by other Massachusetts towns, and the prisoners were eventually supplied with "chequer-boards, combs, stationery, towels, soap, hankerchiefs." One soldier wrote home: "We are now better clothed than the men in the Confederate army, they being ready to purchase any garment we have to sell."

The men on the floor of one building did not lack for funds. The currency, called "shinplasters," then in circulation in the South, was paper money in the form of corporation notes issued by business firms, plank road companies, private banks and other firms. Some men of the 20th Massachusetts discovered a half barrel of this paper, which needed only to be signed. The forgery was accomplished, and a guard was bribed to buy tea, tobacco and other luxuries.

One of the officials of the prisons at this time was a Lieutenant Todd, who was believed by the prisoners to be a halfbrother of Mrs. Lincoln. Another was Henry Wirtz, later commandant of the infamous Andersonville prison, who, after the war, was hanged for his treatment of Union prisoners. At this time, however, there were no direct complaints against him. Todd, on the other hand, was said to have been "grossly insulting," and was accused of striking a sick private with the flat of his sword and of hitting another with the butt end of a musket, but in general there were few complaints of cruel treatment from the men captured at Ball's Bluff until Jefferson Davis decided to use some of them as hostages and threatened to set them swinging on a gallows.

11.
The Hostages
✳ ✳ ✳

For whatever causes the great American Civil War was fought, those who did the fighting, most of them, thought that their own reasons were the right ones—not in pragmatic terms, but inherently, morally right. Certainly this was true of the enthusiastic volunteers, North and South, who in 1861 gaily went off to war cheering. Each was sure that his cause, for which he was willing to risk his life, was a just cause and that he was engaged in a just war.

The political leaders of these men also believed their cause was just, but they were pragmatists and opportunists: Lincoln and Davis, Edwin Stanton and Judah Benjamin, men whose business was war but who were excused from fighting it. They were men of high ideals, all of them, but when forced to choose between pragmatism and idealism, it was always the former that was taken, even at the cost of injustice. It happened sometimes that the soldiers and sailors became helpless pawns in their political maneuverings for the noble causes they represented. So it was that some men of high purpose who had gone off to fight—to preserve the Union or for the "Sacred Cause" of the South—when captured found themselves treated not as legitimate prisoners of war, but as criminals. This was a risk they had not been told about, something they had not bargained for when they volunteered; it was the small print in the contract, a condition added after the signature. Such was the fate of a handful of Confederate sailors and Union army officers who found their futures intertwined in a deadly tangle of loyalties and political expedience.

The trouble started when both Lincoln and Davis began skating along the borders of what most civilized nations consider to be international law. Privateering, the arming of private ships authorized to make war on enemy shipping, had been outlawed by most of the advanced countries of the world by the Declaration of Paris in 1856, but the United States, although observing the Declaration, was not a signatory. In April 1861, two days after Lincoln called for 75,000 volunteers, Davis invited shipowners to apply for letters of marque and reprisal. Lincoln then (April 19) declared a blockade of the Southern ports. This was of questionable legality, for one of the peculiarities of international law is that a declared blockade is legal only when it is enforceable, and it was doubtful indeed if the Union navy of 1861 was yet capable of enforcement. Lincoln's declaration of the blockade carried a warning that anyone molesting a United States ship would be considered a pirate; the traditional punishment for piracy, of course, was death by hanging.

The first major event to agitate the public mind after the Battle of Ball's Bluff occurred on November 8 when Captain John Wilkes in the USS *San Jacinto* boarded the *Trent*, a British mail ship, and carried off James M. Mason and John Slidell, Confederate commissioners bound for Britain. The North cheered and Wilkes was the hero of the hour, but there were cries of indignation in the South and Britain was outraged. England prepared to embark 8,000 regulars for Canada and sent a strongly-worded protest, which arrived in Washington in December. On Christmas Day Lincoln and his cabinet met to consider the matter and wisely concluded that in spite of the popular approval of Wilkes's high-handed action and in spite of the humiliation involved, the commissioners must be set free and Britain appeased. On New Year's Day 1862 Mason and Slidell were put aboard HMS *Rinaldo* at Provincetown and continued on their way to England. So ended the "*Trent* affair." But the North smarted and dreamed of revenge; the means for retribution were at hand.

On May 18, 1861, the Confederacy had issued letters of marque to the *Savannah*, a 53-ton schooner with raking masts, under the command of Captain Thomas Baker, a 37-year-old seaman with a florid face and red beard. The *Savannah* mounted an 18-pounder pivot gun amidships and carried a crew of nineteen. John Harleston, a 28-year-old former Texas rancher, was first mate; Henry Cashman Howard of North Carolina was sailing master; and Charles Sydney Passalaigue, nineteen years old, gave up his job on the Charleston *Mercury* to sail as the *Savannah*'s purser. Not all the crew were patriots, it seems. One of the sailors was Joseph Cruz del Cano, a Spaniard whose home was in England; Del Cano later said that he had been out of work in Charleston and that "necessity not inclination" induced him to ship out on the *Savannah*.

Captain Baker had good luck at the beginning of his voyage. On the morning of June 3, his second day out of port, he captured the brig *Joseph*, en route to Philadelphia from Cuba with a load of sugar. A prize crew of six was put on board to take it into Charleston and the *Savannah* sailed on—but not for long. Later that same day the USS *Perry*, a brig commanded by Lieutenant E.G. Parrott, overtook the *Savannah* and forced her to haul down her flag.

On October 23 (two days after the Battle of Ball's Bluff) Captain Baker and his crew were charged with piracy and put on trial before the United States Circuit Court of the Southern District of New York. The trial lasted eight days; the jury could not agree and was dismissed. During the trial and in the weeks that followed, while the government debated whether or not to have a new trial, the crew of the *Savannah* was confined in the Tombs. In a letter to a friend, which Baker tried unsuccessfully to smuggle out, he wrote that he was in a cell eight feet long and five and a half feet wide. He was allowed to have books and visitors and, he said, was able to get "very good board for about $1 per day or a little over, having my meals just as I order them." He discovered, as many in and out of prison have found, that "with money a person can get along very well." (Captain Baker's letter was discovered on Mr. A.S. Sullivan, one of his lawyers.)

The rest of the *Savannah*'s crew appear not to have fared as well as Baker, for two doctors who visited them reported that their cells were too small, there was not enough air, they were given fresh vegetables infrequently, and that three of the privateers were suffering from "scurvy & pulmonary consumption in consequence of these deprivations, and they will in our opinion soon die."

Meanwhile, Jefferson Davis had written to Lincoln about the privateers. He took note that they were being treated as criminals rather than as prisoners of war, and he gave a grim warning. The Confederates wished to treat prisoners of war with the "greatest justice and leniency," he said, but "if driven to the terrible necessity of retaliation by your execution of any of the officers or crew of the *Savannah*, that retaliation will be extended so far as shall be requisite to secure the abandonment of a practice unknown to the warfare of civilized men, and so barbarous as to disgrace the nation which shall be guilty of it." Lincoln read the letter carefully, but he did not reply.

Davis decided to make his threat more pungent by actually selecting thirteen of the highest ranking Union officers in his prisons to serve as hostages for the thirteen officers and men of the *Savannah*. So on Sunday, November 10, 1861, Brigadier General John H. Winder, Provost Marshal and commander of the prisons in Richmond, together with members of his staff, visited the Mayo tobacco factory for the purpose of selecting those who would be hostages. There were no general officers then in prison and only ten field officers. These ten were automatically selected, but as three more officers were required to equal the number of captured privateers, a grim lottery was held to select three captains. The names of all captains held prisoner were placed in a box and Congressman Ely was asked to draw out three names.

Ely may not have approved of the procedure, but he must have felt relieved, for one of his visitors, a former senator from Texas, had told him that the Confederates intended to hang *him* if the captain of the *Savannah* was convicted; he had already read in the Richmond *Examiner* that he was to be put in a dungeon and kept there until the *Savannah's* crew was released. The Confederates might well have considered "congressman" to be a rank equivalent to a field officer, but they did not.

The casting of lots has often been used by those in authority who wish to or are required to do an evil thing but want to avoid as much responsibility for it as possible, or to ease their consciences of the burden of choice. It is an impersonal method and so has an aura of fairness about it, and it shifts the blame for the choice to the hands of God or the fates.

Those chosen in the draw were George W. Rockwood of the 15th Massachusetts and two others, but when it was learned that the other captains were wounded and in the hospital, new names were drawn and Captain Francis Keffer of the California Regiment and Henry Bowman of the 15th Massachusetts were selected instead. Thus, all of the captains and three of the ten field officers—Colonel Lee, Colonel Cogswell and Major Revere—were prisoners taken at Ball's Bluff.

Four days after the drawing, the hostages were transferred from the tobacco warehouse and factory to the Henrico County Jail, for president Davis had decided that if the privateers were to be treated as common criminals, the hostages would be given the same treatment. Before leaving the factory prison, they said their farewells. Major Revere's last words to his brother, Edward, were: "Remember, whatever happens, it is all right." Colonel Lee wanted to look as smart as he could, and First Sergeant R.H.L. Talcott, Company D, 20th Massachusetts, who had been acting as his orderly, helped him with his toilet and polished his boots. As Lee was about to be taken away, Talcott asked him if there was anything further he could do for him. "No, Sergeant," he replied, "all I want is your best wishes."

"You not only have my best wishes, but the best wishes of all the regiment," said Sergeant Talcott.

Lee, believing that he was sending his last message to his men, cleared his throat and said, "Tell the men . . . " He paused, cleared his throat and tried again: "Tell the men that their colonel died like a brave man." The colonel's words were carried back to his men and eventually to Massachusetts, where they moistened many an eye.

Talcott asked: "Do you think that when our government finds out how we are situated here they will hang those pirates?"

"The government has a policy to carry out and will do it, no matter whose neck stretches," Lee answered.

At the Henrico County Jail the hostages were put together in a ground floor cell seventeen feet by eleven and a half feet with two small barred windows looking out on the yard used as a whipping place for refractory slaves. When they complained of its small size, they were told that "fourteen slaves had been very comfortable there last summer." Their jailor, according to Lee, was a "coarse, ruffianly, drunken sot" who read their mail. Once, when delivering mail to the hostages, he remarked, "Colonel, your wife writes in fine spirits; keep yours up." To the hostages it seemed a shocking thing that their mail was read.

The jail swarmed with rats. Captain Keffer was so terrified of them that he stayed awake nights beating them off. Lee wrote to his adjutant, Charles Peirson:

> *This is indeed a prison. Two meals a day. . . .*
> *Iron grated doors and two high windows. Does the*
> *sun shine? Is it pleasant to look at the sky? A*
> *county jail is not a fit place for men charged with*
> *constructive crimes.*

On November 11 Colonel Cogswell wrote a long letter to his brother-in-law in which, after describing his "painful circumstances," he asked him to comfort his wife, Susan, and to prevent her coming to Richmond under any circumstances. Susan Cogswell had given birth to a daughter only three months before. He wrote:

> *In this pending calamity I feel much more for my wife and my child than myself. I believe that the majority of the officers on the list are married men, with wives and children as dear to them as my Susan and the "Little Lady" are to me. . . .*

> *I never supposed that honestly and faithfully serving my country would bring my neck in danger of a halter, but so it appears. I never thought that being spared the hailstorm of balls at Leesburg, I might have to face death in another and dishonorable form.*

> *Tell S.B. that I expect him to do his best, as I do not wish to be hung for piracy on the high seas, when I have never ventured on the briny deep without being seasick. . . .*

> *What do people say about the exchange of prisoners? The government must exchange or carry the war to extermination. They can take no middle course.*

The "S.B." referred to in the letter was probably Samuel L.M. Barlow, a New York lawyer who was an "old and valued" friend of Cogswell. Barlow's law firm was defending the *Savannah*'s crew, and he had written to Confederate Secretary of War Judah Benjamin to report that the Confederate privateers were being well-treated and to request equal treatment for Cogswell and the other hostages.

Seven junior officers at the tobacco factory, six of whom were Ball's Bluff captives, wrote to the Confederate authorities, offering to change places with seven of the hostages. Their request was refused. Elizabeth Van Lew, a Union sympathizer and spy in Richmond, did what she could to help bring the hostages food and comforts. It is said that she developed a particular attachment to handsome (and married) 28-year-old Major Paul Revere.

Back home, none worked harder to free the thirteen hostages (or at least her husband) than did Adaline Keffer of Philadelphia, wife of Captain Francis Keffer. On December 13 she wrote to Secretary of War Simon Cameron, begging him to release the privateers. Reminding him that she had three children—"one a girl aged nearly 14, a son 12 and one 4 years"—she told him: "My husband writes to me that he is of the firm opinion that if something is not done soon that some of these gentlemen will not be able to bear up under the weight of their troubles." She closed with the plea that her letter be shown to the president. Later she wrote directly to Lincoln—and to everyone else with influence that she could think of. When Edwin Stanton became Secretary of War, she wrote to inquire if she should write to the mayor of New York or to the Tombs to "ask is there anyone there that would exchange for my husband?"

Government leaders in Washington were doing a considerable amount of soul searching as the second year of the war began. They wanted somehow to make up for the government's humiliation in the *Trent* affair and to stick to the threat Lincoln had made to treat privateers as pirates, but satisfying as it might be to hang the crew of the *Savannah*, they knew it would be unpleasant indeed if Jefferson Davis carried out his threat to hang the hostages, as he certainly gave every indication of doing.

To take liberties with captives in war, to treat them harshly or inhumanely, on whatever pretext, is a dangerous game, for two can play. This war, still young, had reached a dangerous corner. In spite of the inflamed passions that swept the land, the war itself had been fought by the soldiers in as civilized a fashion as it was possible to fight a war. There were, of course, atrocity stories. It was said, for example, that Union prisoners at Ball's Bluff had been murdered in cold blood. Such stories were untrue and were generally discounted. Until now, fighting men on both sides had been recognized as legitimate combatants and were treated as such. The desire of politicians to change this threatened to alter the character of the war, to take it down a road towards increasing barbarity, a course which would have created such bitterness and hatred that the wounds could never have been healed. It almost happened. It was a hazardous moment in American history.

The decision was Lincoln's. After the defeats at Manassas and Ball's Bluff, after being forced to return the Confederate commissioners taken off the *Trent*, was it necessary for the president to back off again in the face of Jefferson Davis's threat to retaliate? People said that the North had had about all the humiliation it could stand, and many were asking, as did *Harper's Weekly*, "Will he have the courage to hang the pirate captain?"

Davis was firm, but he was not eager to get into a hanging contest with Lincoln. He thought personal representation might help, so on January 20, 1862, First Lieutenant Charles Peirson, the adjutant of the 20th Massachusetts, was released on parole after signing a promise "upon honor not to communicate in writing or verbally for publication any facts ascertained which if known to the enemy might be injurious to the Confederate States of America."

Although no formal cartel had been as yet negotiated, there were some exchanges of prisoners of war, and a system had been worked out to effect them. At intervals a Union steamer put out from Fortress Monroe and a Confederate steamer from Norfolk; they met half way and the exchange was made in

Chesapeake Bay. Peirson said: "When we saw again the Stars and Stripes we were overpowered with emotion, and fell with streaming eyes upon our knees on the deck, raising our arms to heaven and offering thanks to God for all his mercies."

Again on Union soil, Peirson wasted no time; he hurried to Washington and began lobbying for the release of the Confederate privateers. He talked to every important senator and representative he could reach, wrote Governor Andrew, and, of course, talked with Edwin Stanton, the new Secretary of War. He was persuasive, but it is doubtful that his pleas or the pleas of friends and relations carried much weight with the president. Lincoln, far-sighted and pragmatic, could see the long range political consequences of hanging prisoners and decided that the game would not be worth the candle. On January 31, 1862, he quietly transferred all the privateers to the custody of the War Department. They would henceforth be treated as prisoners of war. Five days later, when the word got back to Richmond, the hostages were taken from the Henrico County Jail and returned to the tobacco factory.

The history of parole and exchange in the Civil War is a sad one: prisoners continued to be used as pawns and much unnecessary suffering resulted. When General Ben Butler executed a Southerner for tearing down the Union flag in New Orleans, Jefferson Davis decreed that no Union officer taken captive would be released on parole or exchanged until Butler was captured and hanged. He backed down, but then Stanton ordered the exchange of officers discontinued. Later, when the Confederates refused to exchange black troops or their white officers, General Grant stopped all exchanges.

The officers and men captured at Ball's Bluff were, after all, fortunate. Although a cartel was not agreed on until July 22, 1862, most were released on giving their parole. On February 24 all of the former hostages, together with Surgeon Revere, four lieutenants and a number of enlisted men captured at Ball's Bluff arrived in Baltimore. The Revere brothers

172

reached Boston on the evening of February 28, and there Major Paul Revere saw for the first time the daughter born while he was in prison.

The Reveres were no longer the gay young officers who only six months earlier had gone off to war. To friends and relations they seemed "worn and old looking, with the strange expression those carry who have been in confinement, or under great pressure of care . . . youth had gone out of them wonderfully . . . and [there were] dull lines about the face that were sad to see."

Although released on parole, most officers had not yet been exchanged and were restrained by their pledged word from returning to the army. Only a change of status from paroled to exchanged could lift the prohibition, and an exchange could only be effected by both sides releasing from all restrictions an equal number of soldiers of equal rank and physical condition.

The officers captured at Ball's Bluff were eager to be exchanged. Major Revere impatiently took matters into his own hands. He went to Fort Warren, where a number of Confederate officers were confined, and selected three prisoners whose ranks corresponded to his own, his brother's and Colonel Lee's. He then persuaded Stanton to allow them to go to Richmond on the understanding that if in fifteen days time the Confederate government had not agreed to the exchange, they would voluntarily return to prison. The Confederate government agreed, and on May 2 the Revere brothers and Colonel Lee were able to rejoin their regiment—in time to see action at Yorktown.

The City of New York, as "a token of appreciation of the services he has rendered and the esteem in which he is held," presented Colonel Milton Cogswell with a handsome sash, belt and a sword costing $500. On its blade was inscribed, "Boys, we will cut our way to Edwards Ferry," the words he had called out after taking command at Ball's Bluff. It was not until September 25, 1862, that Colonel Cogswell was exchanged for Colonel James M. Gee of the 15th Arkansas, captured at Fort Donelson in February 1862. Both could now return to duty.

All but about 150 of the Union enlisted men captured at Ball's Bluff were exchanged in February. One of them was Private Prichard, who had the misfortune to be captured again later in the war and to be sent to Andersonville, where he starved to death. Another was Private William A. Alger of Worcester, Massachusetts. Although captured, Alger considered himself lucky, for at Ball's Bluff a bullet had passed between his shoe and stocking without injuring him. Later in the war he was again captured and again exchanged. Then his luck ran out. Captured a third time, he was sent to Andersonville, where he died. Several Ball's Bluff prisoners had been transferred from Richmond to Salisbury, South Carolina, and on June 1 these too were exchanged.

This early in the war there existed no system for receiving soldiers who were exchanged. Officers were usually eager to rejoin their regiments, but not all the enlisted men were enthusiastic about returning to their units when they reached their own side. Cogswell wrote to Colonel E.D. Townsend, Assistant Adjutant General: "Many I understand have already left for their homes, and I fear unless I have some one to take charge of them that more will leave for their homes."

The nature of prisoner exchange was not always understood by the soldiers or, it seems, by their wives. When the friend of a captured 20th Massachusetts soldier called on his wife with the good news that her husband was soon to be exchanged, she burst into tears and sobbed: "But I love Tom; the children love Tom; and I don't want him exchanged. I won't have a rebel husband, so now!"

There was, besides the privateers and the hostages, at least one other innocent victim of the *Savannah* affair. Horace W. Bridges, the mate of the *Joseph*, which the *Savannah* had captured and sent to Charleston, was kept for three months in a Confederate prison, where his money and all of his clothes, except those he was wearing, were stolen. He was ill when released and spent a month in a Philadelphia hospital. As soon as he recovered, he was arrested by a United States marshal and confined for 108 days in a "house of detention" as a possible witness against the crew of the *Savannah*. When it was decided not to try the privateers again, Bridges was released, still without money and with only the clothes he stood in, and was not paid the customary witness fee he had been promised. He sent an urgent appeal to Secretary Seward, but there is no record that he was ever compensated for his losses. Probably he was not.

12.
The Joint
Committee
✳ ✳ ✳

The military results of the Battle of Ball's Bluff were slight. Evans's victory was a tactical one; the South gained no strategic advantages. There were, however, some psychological effects. The South's overweening sense of its military superiority was enhanced, and perhaps it made McClellan even more cautious and more reluctant to commit his men to battle. But certainly the most enduring and important effect of the battle was its political consequences in Washington.

A week after the battle the New York *Times* reported the "bitter controversy" over who was to blame for the disaster. Partisans of Stone, who tended to be regular officers and their supporters, blamed Baker, whose friends and admirers blamed Stone and were demanding a court of inquiry. "In one instance," wrote the *Times* correspondent, "the regulars intimate that nothing but a defeat could be expected when a movement was entrusted to volunteers, while the volunteers say that every movement is so hampered and embarrassed by the regulars that nothing but disaster can follow. . . . The extent to which this feeling runs is almost incredible."

The first session of the Thirty-Seventh Congress had ended when the North was trying to recover from the shock of the defeat at Bull Run; the second session opened on December 2, 1862, when the nation was still struggling to comprehend the disaster at Ball's Bluff. One of the first acts of the House of Representatives was to pass a resolution, introduced by Roscoe Conklin of New York, that the Secretary of War be asked "whether any, and if any, what measures have been taken to ascertain who is responsible for the disastrous movement of our troops at Ball's Bluff." Conklin labeled Ball's Bluff a "blunder" and intemperately described it as "the most atrocious military murder ever committed in our history as a people."

There is no doubt that the questions raised in the House were reflections of the mood of the congressmen's constituents and that Conklin's feelings were widely shared. Not only the New York *Times*, but newspapers from end to end of the nation were crying "someone has blundered," and demanding to know who. The New York *Evening Post* was typical: "This disgraceful blunder. . .has not yet been explained. Somebody was at fault—General Stone or General McClellan—and justice to the innocent, as well as regard for the safety of our army and our cause, demands that the guilty author of such an affair as this should be exposed, and not only removed but punished."

At first the War Department was reluctant to provide a scapegoat. Not until December 11 did Simon Cameron, the Secretary of War, furnish the House with a reply, and then he merely said that "the General-in-Chief of the Army is of opinion that an inquiry on the subject of the resolution would at this time be injurious to the public service." The House refused to accept this and informed Cameron that his reply was "not responsive or satisfactory to the House." Three days later, on January 9, 1862, Cameron told Galusha A. Grow, Speaker of the House, that "measures have been taken to ascertain who is responsible for the disastrous movement of our troops at Ball's Bluff, but that it was not deemed compatible with the public interest to make known these measures at the present time." But the Congress had already taken steps to discover for itself who was responsible. On December 20,

1861, a resolution was adopted in both houses of Congress to create a committee "to inquire into the conduct of the present war" and Ball's Bluff in particular. The joint committee was to consist of three senators appointed by the vice president, and four representatives appointed by the Speaker of the House.

Thus was formed the Joint Committee on the Conduct of the War, a new and powerful force in government. It was to become the most influential, meddlesome, mischievous and baneful committee in the legislative history of the United States. Nothing quite like it had appeared before and not until nearly a century later, when Senator Joseph McCarthy with equal energy and ruthlessness led his committee in an attack on the United States Army, did a similar phenomenon occur.

At their first meeting the members of the committee agreed to collect such information as would enable them "to advise what mistakes had been made in the past and the proper course for the future." They determined that their interrogations should be held in secret and—most curious for a congressional committee—that they would report their findings, not to the Congress, but to the president and his cabinet, giving "such recommendations and suggestions as seemed to be most imperatively demanded."

The committee was dominated by Radical Republicans, and its chairman was coarse-fibred but politically astute Senator Benjamin Franklin Wade, sixty-one years old. Wade was born on a poverty-stricken farm in western Massachusetts, and he had little formal education—only seven days, according to the Cincinnati *Commercial*. As a young man he had worked as a farm hand, cattle driver and a day laborer on the Erie Canal, but he managed somehow to educate himself and in 1828 was admitted to the Ohio bar. He became a justice of the peace in Ashtabula County and then in succession a prosecuting attorney, state senator, president of the Judicial Circuit, and finally, in 1851, the state legislature elected him

The disaster at Ball's Bluff spawned the scourge known as the Joint Committee on the Conduct of the War. Led by its chairman, Senator Benjamin F. Wade (above), and his crony, Senator Zachariah Chandler (opposite), the committee persistently interfered with the war effort. Ignoring testimony that placed responsibility for the Ball's Bluff defeat on their former colleague Edward Baker, Wade and Chandler instead went after Charles Stone, the most convenient scapegoat. Treating gossip, rumor and opinion as hard fact, they fashioned a ridiculous argument for blaming Stone and doubting his loyalty.

a United States senator. He was short, stocky and deep chested, with keen little eyes and bulldog-like flews, his upper lip lapping over the lower lip at the corners of his mouth. He looked intimidating, and his unpolished manners did nothing to dispel the impression. He never outgrew the rough vocabulary of his early years, and he was known as "Bluff Ben." In debate he was brutal, defiant, profane and blustering. A shrewd, aggressive, fire-eating, table-pounding politician was "Bluff Ben" Wade, and few dared to cross him. In politics he was a Radical Republican and a rabid abolitionist; slavery and the Southern cause had no fiercer opponent.

Wade's crony, and the second most powerful member of the Joint Committee, was Senator Zachariah Chandler of Michigan. He was born in New Hampshire but as a teenager had gone west to seek his fortune, and he had found it. At age twenty he opened a store in Detroit and prospered mightily. He expanded into real estate and became a millionaire. Like Wade, he was an active anti-slavery man; he had fostered the "underground railroad" in Detroit, helping slaves escape into Canada, and in 1856 he had contributed $10,000 toward a fund to provide rifles and supplies to abolitionists in the Kansas civil war. One of the founders of the Republican Party, he had been in the Senate since 1857. He was an intemperate man. When the southern states defected, he told the Senate that he would sell his store and all his land and go live with the Comanches rather than live in a Union that was "a rope of sand," and in a private letter, which caused a commotion when it was made public, he said that "without a little blood-letting the Union was not worth a rush." He was a tough, bloody-minded zealot.

The third senator on the original committee was a Democrat: Andrew Johnson, the future president. He had never attended school but at eighteen had married a 16-year-old girl who taught him to read and write; with these skills he made himself into a lawyer and politician, becoming mayor, congressman, governor of Tennessee and in 1857 a United States senator. His constituency consisted of the Tennessee mountain people who kept no slaves and were loyal to the Union. Johnson remained on the Joint Committee only a short time.

Lincoln appointed him military governor of Tennessee on March 4, 1862, and his place was taken successively by J.A. Wright of Indiana, B.F. Harding of Oregon, and finally by C.R. Bucklaw of Pennsylvania.

The four members from the House of Representatives were John Covode of Pennsylvania (later succeeded by B.F. Loam of Missouri), Moses F. Odell (a combative Democrat from Brooklyn), D.W. Gooch of Massachusetts, and George W. Julian of Indiana. In the proceedings of the Committee, all followed the lead of Bluff Ben Wade and "Zach" Chandler; none protested the Star Chamber methods they employed.

The Joint Committee on the Conduct of the War existed until June 1865, and in the course of its activities it ranged far and wide. The Committee sat in a room in the basement of the Capitol, and to this room were summoned civilians, bureaucrats and soldiers of every rank from private to major general, including every commanding general of the Army of the Potomac except U.S. Grant. The Committee at various times demanded maps showing the location of all troops, correspondence between officers, and plans for campaigns. They recommended organizational changes in the army and otherwise interfered in strictly military affairs. On January 23, 1862, they told Secretary of War Stanton that in their opinion the army had enough cavalry. As cavalry was more expensive than infantry, "in view of the financial condition of the country," new cavalry regiments being raised should be "dispensed with at once," they said.

The committeemen revelled in campfire gossip, accepted hearsay evidence, and frequently asked lieutenants and captains their opinions of their superiors and of their general's conduct of a battle. Junior officers were flattered when Wade would begin his question with, "Is it good generalship for a general officer to . . . ?" or "What is your judgment as a military man . . . ?" And even when, as was frequently the case, the "military man" had been in uniform for only a few months, the Committee listened solemnly to his opinions when those opinions corresponded to their own suspicions or prejudices.

High military rank did not awe them and generals were questioned like "refactory schoolboys." Indeed, the Committee was soon making recommendations to Lincoln and his secretary of war as to generals they thought should be removed and those they thought should be promoted. Wade and Chandler were particularly suspicious of generals who were Democrats; they tended to equate differences of political opinion with treason. They had been in favor of deposing old General Scott and replacing him with McClellan, but not long after McClellan was given command of the Army of the Potomac, they turned on "Little Mac" and clamored for his head.

When Wade demanded to know why McClellan did not at once march out and fight the rebels, McClellan explained that there were only two bridges across the Potomac to Alexandria and that these were insufficient to safeguard a retreat. Chandler interrupted him: "General McClellan, if I understand you correctly, before you strike at the rebels you want to be sure of plenty of room so you can run in case they strike back."

"Or in case you get scared," sneered Wade.

When McClellan had left the room, Chandler turned to Wade: "I don't know much about war, but it seems to me that this is infernal, unmitigated cowardice."

Wade agreed, and called on Lincoln to tell him that McClellan ought to be replaced. "With whom?" asked Lincoln.

"Anybody," Wade replied.

"Wade," sighed Lincoln, "anybody will do for you, but I have to have somebody."

The Joint Committee's sessions were not only secret, witnesses were forbidden to tell anyone of their testimony. When General George Meade wanted to know what General Alfred

Pleasonton had told the Committee, Pleasonton was quite willing that he be told and asked the Committee to permit Meade to see his testimony, but Wade refused, writing:

> *Being clothed by Congress with all its power in the premises, their own self respect and dignity will not permit them to acknowledge the right of any person to question their authority to examine any one upon any subject which they have been authorized and directed to investigate. In order to do that, every witness must feel himself perfectly free to answer any interrogations the Committee may ask, or to give any testimony which may relate to the subject upon which he may be examined.*

The inquisitors sniffed everywhere for treason, and sometimes they thought they smelled it in high places. Mary Lincoln was unpopular in many quarters, and a rumor circulated that she was writing letters to people in the South. The Joint Committee thought they should investigate until the day the president arrived unannounced at the Capitol and assured them that he was certain no member of his family was engaged in treasonable correspondence with the enemy. The day was not far distant when Wade would openly attack the president, but at this point the investigation of Mrs. Lincoln was quietly dropped.

The possibility of treason was perhaps not far from the minds of the Committee members when on December 27, 1861, they began their investigation of the disaster at Ball's Bluff by calling as their first witness Brigadier General F. W. Lander, who commanded a brigade in Stone's division. Lander testified that he could have taken Leesburg in spite of the presence of masked Confederate batteries that were thought to be between Edwards Ferry and the town. He had been of a mind to steal 3,000 men and take the town, he said. "It is true that, as there were two generals there who outranked me, I should have been broken. I could have done it, I think. At least it shows I did not think much of their batteries."

Lander had been in Washington on the day of the battle and had not returned to Edwards Ferry until the next day, so he had no personal knowledge of the fight. When asked his opinion of General Stone, he testified: "I regard General Stone . . . as a very efficient, orderly, and excellent officer."

Lander was followed the next day by General McCall, who said that "had I been ordered forward, I have not the slightest doubt that I could have defeated Evans and captured his whole command. But it certainly would have been a delicate matter, because they could have thrown up 20,000 or 30,000 men from Centreville and cut off my retreat from Dranesville."

The third person to appear before the Committee and testify on Ball's Bluff was General Charles P. Stone, the most likely scapegoat. McClellan had just succeeded Winfield Scott as general-in-chief on November 1, and he was at the height of his popularity; Baker had been one of their own, a senator, and he was now a dead hero; this left Stone. There had already been criticism of Stone in the press and in the Congress; some had even accused him of murder, saying that he deliberately sent his soldiers to their deaths. This talk was stirred up primarily by Baker's son and brother, aided by the mischievous Captain Francis Young, who in defending Baker had launched an attack on Stone.

Immediately after the battle, Lieutenant Colonel A. V. Colburn, Assistant Adjutant General, had gone up from Washington to Edwards Ferry. On his return he was interviewed by the Washington *Star*, which quoted him as saying that Baker had disobeyed orders when he crossed the river. As a rebuttal, the New York *Daily Tribune* on November 5 published an exceptionally long article, covering a page and a half, written by George Wilkes. Captain Young had found a copy of Baker's orders, covered with blood and brains, in

Baker's hat. The copy of this document was given by Young, at the suggestion of Baker's son and his brother, to Wilkes. The text, however, was altered by unknown hands to support the view that Baker had been ordered to cross. Wilkes's description of the battle placed on Stone the entire blame for the Union defeat. Stone, Young claimed, had given Baker a direct order to cross the river and take Leesburg, at which, he said, Baker exclaimed: "I will obey General Stone's orders, but it is my death-warrant."

Stone did not reply in the press, but although McClellan had on October 24 written that "The disaster was caused by errors committed by the immediate commander [i.e. Baker] not General Stone," he sent McClellan a letter (through General Seth Williams) in which he defended himself, put the blame squarely on Baker, and denounced Baker's "friends":

> It was my strongly expressed desire that, if a respectable force should threaten, this one [Devens'] should be withdrawn, and Colonel Baker left me at Edwards Ferry with a full knowledge of my desire and with full power to withdraw it. . . .

> It has been asserted and published that Colonel Baker received an order from me to attack Leesburg on Sunday the 20th. It is absurd. . . . The plain truth is that this brave and impetuous officer was determined at all hazards to bring on an action, and made use of the discretion allowed him to do it.

With this controversy as a background, the Joint Committee began to inquire into Stone's part in the affair. On January 5 the Joint Committee interrogated him for the first time. It would be difficult to imagine two more disparate men than Charles P. Stone and Benjamin Franklin Wade, the West Point graduate and the ex-navvy, the gentleman who spoke in measured tones and the politician who used language like a sabre to cut and slash. It was only natural that there should be little mutual understanding and a distaste on the part of each for the other. It was Stone's misfortune that they should meet in Wade's lair, where the grand inquisitor was surrounded by like-minded politicians and clothed in the authority of the Congress. Although Stone was a fly caught in the web of a voracious and esurient spider, he appears not to have realized his danger.

Stone's military education was worse than useless; it was a handicap. There was a prejudice in the North against West Pointers and a feeling that they had been given too many high commands that ought to be held by volunteers. Such was the view of Ben Wade and Zach Chandler. Stone's ignorance of political powers and of the skills of politicians increased his vulnerability. He believed in justice, the Articles of War and due process of law; he did not realize that all these could be set aside. He believed in the power of the army to protect him from those outside it who were critical of the methods by which he discharged his duties; he had yet to learn that in this republic powerful armies and their generals were the servants of their political masters, required to do their bidding. Charles Stone was an educated man, but he had much to learn about political processes.

He knew, of course, that some blamed him for the defeat at Ball's Bluff, and he must have known that the country and the Congress were looking for someone on whom to fasten the blame; he must also have been aware that to put the blame where it belonged, on the popular Ned Baker, would be difficult; and he most certainly knew that he had at least one powerful enemy in the Senate. Yet he appears to have been confident that if he was honest with the Joint Committee he could clear his own name. Logic was on his side, but logic has little influence on emotions, and in this instance, as he was to discover, small power to alter suspicions. He faced

Wade and the other members of the Committee with self-confidence and a touch of arrogance.

In retrospect it is easy to see that Stone erred in giving Baker the command at Ball's Bluff. He also erred in not pushing Gorman's brigade northward out of the Edwards Ferry bridgehead to link up with the force on top of the bluff. But Stone could not have known Baker's defects as a commander, and he believed that hidden batteries and superior numbers of infantry stood between Gorman and Ball's Bluff; besides, he had no hint of a disaster until it had occurred. Stone might also be blamed for the lack of sufficient boats in this first amphibious operation of the war, and indeed he ought to have made provision for more to be sent to Harrison's Island, but Baker had the option of withdrawing the small force under Devens and Lee if he believed that his water transportation was inadequate. It can also be argued that had the boats been properly managed, had Baker used them to pass over infantry instead of artillery and its horses, and, of course, had Baker made better disposition of his men, the Union forces might have won. Human errors caused by ignorance are of two kinds: those made through unavoidable ignorance because there is no opportunity to learn the truth or to acquire the necessary facts, and those made when the knowledge necessary to avoid mistakes is available but neglected or ignored. The errors of Stone were generally in the former category; those of Baker in the latter.

As fully, honestly and accurately as he could, Stone laid before the Committee all of Baker's mistakes: his failure to cross over at once to the Virginia shore or even to ask for a report from the battlefield; sending over cannons with their horses; his poor disposition of the infantry and guns; the poor management of the boats. "The whole story," he said, "is that Colonel Baker chose to bring on a battle. He brought it on and, I am sorry to say, handled his troops unskillfully in it, and a disaster occurred which ought not to have occurred."

The members of the Joint Committee gave him their attention. Their questions were critical but not accusatory. If they doubted his loyalty, they gave no hint of it; Stone's suspicions were not aroused. But there can be little doubt that Wade, Chandler and the rest of the Committee scented their prey. Almost all subsequent witnesses were asked about Stone, and the Committee listened attentively to malicious gossip, unfounded rumors, opinions, hearsay and the suspicions of disgruntled soldiers.

On January 10, 1862, the Committee took the testimony of Colonel George W.B. Tompkins, who commanded the 2nd New York State Militia (later renamed the 82nd New York). His testimony is worth examining, for he was the only senior officer to damn Stone. He told the Committee:

> It is said that he receives and sends communications back and forth across the river. In fact, my officers have told me that they have sent, by his orders, letters across the river—sealed letters—and have received sealed letters from the other side, directed to him; that they have received men from the other side, purporting to be spies; that he has ordered women to be sent across, and has sent flags of truce across for others to come over to this side. . . .

> There is not a man in my regiment that will fight under him, if they can avoid it; not one. In fact, they all want to get up a petition to be removed from his division, and I was going down to the hotel this afternoon to see General Dix [John Adam Dix, a former senator from New York] to see if we cannot get out of General Stone's division into General Dix's division.

"Why do you want to get out of General Stone's division?" he was asked.

"Well, sir, for several reasons," said Tompkins. "In the first place, we do not know whether he is what he seems to be; in the next place, we do not think he is as good an officer as he has been represented to be. In fact, we have no confidence in him."

"No confidence in his skill as a general, or in his loyalty?" asked a committee member.

"Both," Tompkins replied.

The Committee was much taken with Colonel Tompkins. Wade asked him: "How come your army [sic] to be infected with the idea that General Stone was disloyal?"

Tompkins's reply was that all citizens of Maryland, where Stone's division was stationed, had a good opinion of him: "They are all very friendly towards him, and think there is no such man as General Stone."

Many northerners put very little trust in the allegiance of the Maryland populace as a whole. The Committee seemed to regard Tompkins's statement as pretty solid proof of Stone's disloyalty. Tompkins readily supplied further evidence equally substantial: "I heard one officer, in my own camp, say distinctly that General Stone was a secessionist, and he would stake his existence on it."

The Committee did not bother to look closely into the character of its witnesses. Two months after giving his testimony, Tompkins was arrested and in May he was discharged from the service as unfit to be an officer.

On the same day Tompkins gave his testimony, two other officers from his regiment, First Lieutenant Philip J. Downey and Captain Dennis de Courcy, also testified. Both spoke of letters and packages crossing the Potomac and of a woman who was allowed to cross from Maryland into Virginia. Downey, an ex-sailor, testified that Stone tried to return slaves to their owners in Virginia. He had read some of the letters that had passed back and forth, he said, but had been unable to find anything incriminating in them. Nevertheless, he told the Committee: "Well, sir, I am an independent character, and speak my mind generally . . . and I generally say what I think." As to General Stone, he said: "I have . . . told all my officers that I thought he was more of a secesh than anything else."

De Courcy agreed, "It is the general opinion that he is not loyal," he said. He testified that all of the officers disliked and distrusted Stone, and they disliked his orders. Asked what orders? he replied, "Well, sir, there was an order read on parade last Saturday or Sunday, stating that the government had trusted us with arms to protect the citizens of Maryland, and that we were getting paid for that duty. I had a copy of that order, but I forgot to bring it with me. It was a perfect insult to the officers and men of his command."

Colonel Wistar was the first officer who had actually fought at Ball's Bluff to appear before the Committee. Although he had been a close friend of Baker's and his former law partner, he insisted that it was Baker rather than Stone who was responsible for the debacle. Wistar declared that he knew of no messages crossing the river other than those concerning the burial of the dead and letters to prisoners of war after the battle. Wade asked if there were any suspicions of Stone or any general feeling that he was disloyal.

"No sir," Wistar replied. "There is no suspicion of any kind; not among any of the troops that I have any connection with; no such idea at all. I think I can safely say that in the brigade to which I belong . . . there is not a man of any rank who has such a feeling."

Wade: "They have confidence in him?"

Wistar: "Yes, sir. Full confidence in him."

The Committee chose to ignore Wistar's testimony and to believe Colonel Tompkins and his officers. At seven o'clock that evening three of the congressmen—Chandler, Gooch and Odell—called on Secretary of War Cameron to tell him of their suspicions of General Stone.

The next witness to appear before the Committee was the

mischief-making Francis G. Young on January 16. Although Young was introduced as "Captain," he had been cashiered exactly two weeks earlier, a fact of which the Committee was ignorant or which it chose to ignore. Young said only: "I got into some trouble with General Stone because I stated pretty freely to the president and the members of the cabinet and to General Scott what my opinion of the battle was."

Young testified that "General Stone is very popular with all the secession people of Maryland there" and that "General Stone is pretty unanimously regarded as not a true, loyal man." He had heard, he said, that the 15th Massachusetts could not obtain recruits because men did not want to serve under him. He added that only recently had Stone flown a flag in front of his tent.

Senator Chandler expressed his shock: "The headquarters of the commanding general?"

Young: "Yes sir."

Wade: "Is not that unusual?"

Young: "I never heard of such a thing."

Most of the adverse testimony came from men in Colonel Tompkins's disaffected regiment, but Captain Clinton Berry of that regiment disappointed the Committee. He said that he had "heard nothing that would indicate that General Stone had any disloyal feeling" and "in regard to my own opinion of General Stone, I think he is certainly one of the most accomplished soldiers and gentlemen that I have ever had the pleasure to meet." Significantly, Berry added: "Our colonel and General Stone are not on very good terms."

Another man with a grudge against Stone was ex-Captain James Brady, formerly of Colonel Tompkins's regiment. He was a contractor who had asked for a furlough to go home and attend to some personal business. When Stone refused to give him leave, he resigned his commission. Even so, he complained, he had lost $3,000 by not getting home soon enough. Much was made of the letters that passed back and forth across the river and Brady told the Committee that he opened all the letters and read them. Asked if they were treasonable, he replied:

> They were treasonable in character, certainly; no doubt about that. But there was no information except personal: that such and such persons were alive and well; that such and such were killed in the action at Bull Run, etc.

Lieutenant Church Howe of the 15th Massachusetts was also asked about the letters. He said he had been across the Potomac three or four times under a flag of truce and had seen some of the correspondence: "there was nothing but letters to our prisoners in Richmond . . . and also some letters over to persons on the other side who have friends on this side. . . . There was nothing in them that would give information."

James Boyle, a former private in Tompkins's regiment, testified that while on picket duty near Edwards Ferry on December 23 he had seen Stone talk with rebel officers under a flag of truce. Although there was nothing secret about the meeting and there were other soldiers about, ex-private Boyle thought it was suspicious, particularly since Stone was given papers of some sort and since he had not explained what he was doing or why. To Ben Wade it seemed most peculiar that the general commanding a division failed to explain his actions to a private on picket duty.

Colonel Tompkins and most of his officers made much of Stone's affable relations with Marylanders. Many echoed Major J.J. Dimmick of the 2nd New York Militia who told the Committee: "The secessionists in the neighborhood always speak in the highest terms of General Stone." That it was in the interest of Stone's command and of the Union cause to keep on friendly terms with the people among whom the troops were camped appears never to have occurred to these officers or to members of the Committee.

Although ostensibly investigating the Battle of Ball's Bluff, the Committee's questions were increasingly directed toward collecting evidence alleging Stone was disloyal. Wade found it suspicious that Stone had not used his guns to destroy mills on the Virginia shore. Philip Haynes, a grain distributor who lived near Edwards Ferry, was called to testify and was asked military questions. "Do you know why that mill is suffered to remain there and grind grain for the rebels?" asked Wade. Haynes had no idea.

Not until January 27 did the Committee call Colonel Charles Devens, the senior surviving officer left on the Union side after Ball's Bluff. The Committee allowed him to describe the battle; then they asked about Stone. Devens stated that he and his officers had complete confidence in General Stone. The Committee ignored him. Wade, Chandler and company had already made up their minds: Stone was a traitor.

13.
The Arrest
of General Stone

✳✳✳

The eleven weeks between the Battle of Ball's Bluff and Stone's appearance before the Joint Committee on the Conduct of the War were busy and tempestuous ones for him. He was troubled by the criticism leveled at him, the rumors that buzzed about, and the falsehoods about his part in the ordering of the battle. The tale retailed by Young, that Baker had said he would obey General Stone's order although it was his death warrant, was widely believed. However, his superiors knew that the fault was Baker's, and the War Department had no intention of holding a court of inquiry.

When, however, on December 2, 1861, Congressman Roscoe Conklin spoke in the House and offered a resolution that the Secretary of War be asked if steps were being taken to determine who was responsible for the disaster of Ball's Bluff, he took occasion to criticize Stone severely. On hearing of this speech, Stone telegraphed McClellan's headquarters and asked if he should demand a court of inquiry. McClellan replied: "Write nothing. Say nothing. Keep quiet." It was sound advice. Now was the time to keep his mouth shut and his head low until the storm subsided, until the horrors of other, bigger battles occupied the public's attention. Now was the time to cultivate his friends in the Congress and cement his friendships with other politicians. But the attacks increased in virulence and became more than he could bear. He lashed out at his tormentors. In doing so, he managed to make enemies of one of the most powerful of state governors and one of the most influential of United States senators, and he raised two troubling issues concerning political-military relationships, which were as yet unresolved: How was the army to consider slaves who one way or another attached themselves to Union army units? And what control did the state governments have over the regiments they raised for federal service?

The Fugitive Slave Law was still on the books, and although in the summer of 1861 the Congress had determined that fugitive slaves were no part of the business of the army, they presented problems that not only divided soldiers and politicians, but caused serious dissension within the army. There were degrees of opinion in the North regarding blacks, ranging from the view that the institution of slavery should be retained and that slaves, being private property, should be returned to their owners if they strayed, to the belief that not only should slaves be freed but that they should be armed to fight against the Confederacy. Freedom for all slaves was not yet a part of the cause to be fought for, though there were politically powerful men who were trying to make it so.

Lincoln, ever the practitioner of *realpolitik*, knew that citizens in the border states and many further north as well did not want to see the institution of slavery abolished, and that even among those who disapproved of it, there were strong objections to putting arms in the hands of Negroes. Lincoln certainly did not want to do anything which would disturb the uncertain loyalties in the border states, and at this stage he still hoped that the war could be won without ripping the social fabric of the South. Freeing slaves and arming them would, he knew, stiffen the Southern will to resist and make it more difficult to recruit volunteers in the North, for although there were many who were willing to risk their lives to preserve the Union, there were considerably fewer willing to fight to free the slaves. Lincoln did not want to rock the boat. He was angry when Secretary of War Cameron advocated the use of black soldiers, and he severely rebuked General John Fremont in Missouri and General David Hunter on the Carolina coast for proclaiming the abolition of slavery in their military districts.

Opinions in the army reflected those in the population as a whole. McClellan told Lincoln that he doubted his troops would fight if the conflict turned into a war against the practice of slavery and that its abolition should not be "contemplated for a moment." But many officers were ardent abolitionists, and throughout the first year and a half of the war there were incidents.

A company commander of the 33rd Illinois, serving in Missouri, one day captured a handful of Confederates on a plantation; he gave rifles to some of the plantation slaves and told them to march the prisoners back to the Union camp. For this he was reprimanded, for he had done "what the president of the United States had not seen fit to do—liberate and arm the slaves." When Major General Don Carlos Buell, commanding a division in the Army of the Potomac, ordered fugitive slaves turned out of his lines, Colonel Henry Briggs, commanding the 10th Massachusetts, wrote him a point blank refusal, and all of General Ormsby Mitchel's officers came to his headquarters to declare that they would not obey Buell's orders; Mitchel himself protested directly to Secretary of War Stanton. Brigadier General Thomas Williams, commanding a brigade in the lower Mississippi, felt himself legally bound to return slaves, and he too clashed with his abolitionist officers. Colonel Halbert E. Paine of the 4th Wisconsin refused to turn slaves out of his camp, and Colonel Frederick W. Curtenius of the 6th Michigan refused to admit slave hunters to his lines.

On Christmas Day, 1861, Brigadier General U.S. Grant, commanding the District of Cairo (Illinois), wrote to Colonel

John Cook, commanding Fort Holt, Kentucky, stating that although he had given permission to a slave owner named Mercer to go to Fort Holt to recover his fugitive slaves, Mercer had complained that he was "forcibly prevented from recovering his property." If this was true, Grant concluded, it was "treating the law, the orders of the Comdr of the Dept. and my orders with contempt. . . . I do not want the Army used as negro cathers [sic], but still less do I want to see it used as a cloak to cover their escape. . . . I direct therefore that you have a search made . . . and if hereafter you find any have been concealed or detained you bring the party so detaining them to punishment."

The most ardent abolitionists in the army, taking their cue from their state governor, were the volunteers in the Massachusetts regiments. Stone, whose division in southern Maryland had three regiments of Massachusetts volunteers, was from the first in a sensitive position. He had encountered problems almost immediately on taking command, and on August 22, 1861, he had queried McClellan: "Five negroes crossed the river yesterday, running away, as they say, from being sent to Manassas to work on the fortifications. I respectfully ask instructions as to the disposition to be made of them." A month before the Battle of Ball's Bluff, in general Order No. 16, Stone had admonished his troops "not to incite and encourage insubordination among the colored servants in the neighborhood of the camps." But the Union camps were an attraction to the slaves in Maryland, and slaves from northern Virginia sometimes slipped across the Potomac and found a sympathetic refuge in the lines of the Massachusetts regiments. Stone tried to steer a legalistic course, aiding neither slaves nor slave hunters, but trouble was probably inevitable.

In the course of the Battle of Ball's Bluff, undoubtedly in the early morning, scouts of the 20th Massachusetts on the Virginia shore encountered two slaves belonging to John Smart, owner of the mill located on the Potomac just above

Ball's Bluff. To prevent the slaves from revealing the Union positions, or perhaps with the notion of freeing them, the soldiers ordered them into a boat and they were carried over into Maryland. After the battle, Smart wrote to Stone, saying he believed the slaves had been carried off against their will and asking that they be allowed to return. The slaves were questioned. Yes, they were indeed anxious to return; their wives and children were in Virginia; Mr. Smart had always been good to them.

When an attempt was made to return them under a flag of truce, the Confederates refused to accept them, perhaps because Smart had something of a reputation among his neighbors of being a Union sympathizer. Brought back to Maryland they settled themselves outside Stone's headquarters for a time and were fed there. No guards were placed over them, and they were treated as free men. Eventually they wandered off. Such was the account given by Stone two years later, and it is substantially confirmed by Lieutenant Richard Derby in a letter he wrote home. However, some Massachusetts soldiers, who saw the slaves carried across the river to the Virginia shore under a flag of truce, concluded that Stone was returning them against their will to their Confederate owners. Their indignant letters to home newspapers and to their governor, added to the stories that Stone was responsible for the defeat at Ball's Bluff, the charge that he returned fugitive slaves to their rebel masters. Lieutenant Derby wrote of Stone: "Half the lies that are told, if they were truths, would have sunk him long ago; and now they have saddled the 'everlasting nigger' upon him."

It is not clear whether the alleged return of Smart's slaves or the rumor of another incident triggered Stone's quarrel with Governor John Andrew of Massachusetts and Massachusetts's U.S. Senator Charles Sumner. The record here is murky. But what is believed is often more important than what occurred, and the story heard and believed by Governor

Andrew was that First Lieutenant George N. Macy, 20th Massachusetts, with a squad of soldiers had, on Stone's orders, taken slaves found in camp and turned them over to their owners. Governor Andrew was highly incensed. He had just signed, on November 8, his approval of the promotion of Macy to captain and he was now sorry he had done so. Through his military secretary, Thomas Drew, he directed a stinging rebuke to Lieutenant Colonel Francis Winthrop Palfrey, who, after Colonel Lee's capture, had assumed command of the 20th Massachusetts:

> *Lieutenant (now captain) Macy has subjected Massachusetts citizen soldiers to the disgrace of becoming kidnappers of their fellow men and returning them into the hands of persons claiming to be their owners without any observance of even the forms of law, either civil or military. His excellency is greatly pained that the fame of your gallant regiment should have been tarnished by an act on the part of one of its officers, the details of which if correctly reported to him prove him to be unworthy of any position of honor, trust or responsibility in her service or in the service of the Federal Government, and he earnestly hopes that your influence will be exerted to save and protect the soldiers of Massachusetts from any such dirty and despotic work in the future, and humanity itself from such infractions under color of military law and duty.*

> *His excellency also directs me to add that you will oblige him by saying to Captain Macy that had he been informed of his discreditable conduct . . . he would never have signed his commission for promotion, which was here . . . about the time this infamous procedure is said to have happened.*

Palfrey was an abolitionist and the son of an active abolitionist father, but he was in the army now and he was not sure what he should do. Doubtless he felt the strain of divided loyalties: to his state and to the army; to his state's governor and to the president. He showed the letter to Stone.

On December 15, 1861, Stone passed on Andrew's letter to Brigadier General Seth Williams, McClellan's assistant adjutant general, along with a protest at this interference with his command: "I do not feel it is consistent with my sworn duty to permit any governor to give orders affecting the discipline of any regiment which the government of the nation has intrusted to my command." Thus was raised the second major issue: the amount of control, if any, which state governors could exercise over their state's troops after they had passed into federal service.

McClellan strongly supported Stone. On December 20 he sent Governor Andrew a copy of Stone's letter and added one of his own in which he stated: "The Volunteer regiments . . . when accepted into the service of the United States become a portion of the Federal Army. . . . As discipline in the service can only be maintained by the strictest observance of military subordination, nothing could be more detrimental than that any interference should be allowed the constituted authorities."

Andrew shot back a spirited reply on Christmas Eve. He reminded McClellan that Massachusetts had raised the regiments, clothed them, armed them and completely equipped them, "down to shoe-strings and tent-pins." He protested that he had not given orders to Palfrey, but had only requested that he comply with his wishes, and he noted pointedly that he was responsible for filling all vacancies in the regiments, and he accused McClellan of injuring the service "by interrupting the proper relations between Massachusetts colonels and their governor."

McClellan, wanting to be sure of his ground, asked for an opinion from J.F. Lee, the judge-advocate. Lee gave his opinion in no uncertain terms:

> He [Andrew] attempts too fine a point when he deduces his right to revile captains and instruct colonels from the power to appoint; it is a simple absurdity which may not unpleasantly be pointed out to him. His doctrine is worse than a Trojan horse to any walled town. . . . The Boston Courier, an able paper, attacked him and justified Stone out and out. . . . There is danger in that abolition element unless a little energy check it at the start.

Armed with this advice, McClellan again wrote to Governor Andrew. His forceful letter lacked tact:

> I am of opinion that as the governor of a State holds no authority over the volunteers in the service of the United States he is not warranted in assuming any such function for any purpose, and the exercise of it . . . must be very mischievous.

> In this case you inform the officers that certain acts done "under color of military law and duty" were "dirty and despotic work," "disreputable conduct," "infamous procedure." The acts your excellency so warmly and vehemently denounces were acts under cognizance of the military authority of the United States which that authority is competent to order or forbid, to approve or punish; and which if it approves it cannot permit any other authority to denounce to the troops or censure in any way that may tend to excite disobedience or disaffection. The volunteer troops from the States must obey according to the rules and discipline of war the officers appointed over them by the United States. The reg-

> *imental commanders must not accept nor convey to*
> *the officers or soldiers under them any denunciation*
> *or any advice, opinion or suggestion from the State*
> *authorities in censure of the orders and duty im-*
> *posed by the United States; and any commander or*
> *other person subject to discipline so offending will*
> *be liable to answer to a court-martial under the*
> *mutiny articles of war for inciting mutiny and sedi-*
> *tion.*

Stone and McClellan were right, of course; the army could not function if its officers had to obey both their state governors and their commanding officers, but being right does not turn one's antagonist into a friend. Andrew abandoned his argument with McClellan and returned to the original issue, taking a different tack. Politicians have a variety of weapons in their arsenals, and some are those not generally available to ordinary citizens or to generals. Andrew had already written to Senator Charles Sumner, enclosing the correspondence and asking him to cooperate in his efforts "to protect the soldiers of Massachusetts from being made the bloodhounds of slavery in obedience to the iniquitous and illegal orders of brigadier generals, and others in the interest of slave power." Sumner, as ardent an abolitionist as Andrew, responded by launching a vicious attack upon Stone from the floor of the Senate.

Charles Sumner (1811–1874), a humorless, doctrinaire abolitionist, was one of the most influential and best known men in the Senate. He was a powerful and polished orator whose skills as a denouncer had often been demonstrated during the ten years he had served. He was clothed in an arrogance that admitted no self-doubt, and he was a dangerous man to have as an enemy. Politically astute, Sumner realized that it would not be wise to attack the still popular McClellan, but he knew he could be reached through his subordinate, a non-political brigadier general whose professional reputation had already been tarnished by the failure of his troops at Ball's Bluff.

When Stone at Poolesville read an account of the speech in the *National Intelligencer*, he exploded in fury. Although naturally a quiet, reserved man, of whom it was said that he "thought before he spoke," he obviously did not think long enough before he sat down on December 23 to write in his firm, clear hand a note to Sumner, accusing him of having uttered "*a slander* and *a falsehood*." It was a short letter, but it was long enough to reveal his frustration, anger and sense of injustice:

> *Please accept my thanks for your speech in which you use my name.*
>
> *There can hardly be better proof that a soldier in the field is faithfully performing his duty, than the fact that while he is receiving the shot of the public enemy in front he is at the same time receiving the vituperation of a well known coward from a safe distance in the rear.*

This was not the kind of letter which could do Stone any possible good, and it most certainly could do him harm. If he meant to provoke a duel, he failed. Sumner's weapons were words, not pistols; his arena was the Senate floor, not an open field at dawn. Sumner showed Stone's intemperate letter to those of his friends, certain to be angered by it. He took it to president Lincoln, too, but Lincoln proved a disappointment: "I don't know that I would have written such a letter," he said mildly, "but if I wanted to, I think, under the circumstances—under the circumstances, mind you—I would have had a right to do so."

It would have been far wiser, of course, for Stone to have sought a meeting with Sumner or to have written a letter explaining his position and his views, or simply to have done nothing. When on January 5, 1862, he was questioned by the Joint Committee on the Conduct of the War, Senator Wade mentioned Sumner's speech and the newspaper reports that claimed Stone returned slaves to secessionists. To this Stone made a spirited reply:

> *That is a slander that has been circulated very freely. . . . I have insisted upon my troops obeying every law of the state of Maryland. I do not allow them to harbor the slaves, or the free employed negroes, or the apprentices, or the sons or daughters of the farmers in the neighborhood of my camps. If a negro runs away from a farmer into my camps and lounges around there, he is turned out of the camps. If they come along the borders of the camps selling whiskey to the soldiers, they are treated precisely as white men are: they are taken and whipped and sent away just as white men are. . . . The slaves that run away from the enemy and come over are got to my head-quarters as rapidly as possible; they are there questioned carefully, and all the information I can get out of them is taken. They are made as comfortable as they can be, and put to work in the quartermaster's department, or have been until lately. . . . I am not aware of any slaves coming over from the enemy's lines having been given up to any claimant.*

Congressman Julian asked: "Do you give up slaves when they are pursued by the claimants?" Stone again explained that he never had done so, but that he had no authority to declare martial law and that he was required to obey the laws of Maryland. Stone's logic was incontestable and it certainly conformed to Lincoln's views, but it was not an answer which satisfied abolitionist politicians such as Wade and Chandler.

Stone appears to have feared no evil as a result of his testimony before the Joint Committee. He even took the opportunity to complain of the bad effect on discipline caused by Senator Sumner's attack on him. "I have had in my own camps soldiers . . . discussing what their senator says of the commanding general," he said indignantly.

Since the primary purpose of the Joint Committee and the reason for calling Stone before it was to inquire into the disaster at Ball's Bluff, Stone was questioned about his role. He may have thought he satisfactorily answered all the Committee's questions about the battle, but he was less than candid, for that very morning he had been told at McClellan's headquarters of McClellan's desire that "officers giving testimony before the Committee should not state, without his authority, anything regarding his plans, his orders for the movement of troops, or his orders concerning the position of troops," and Stone had understood this to mean all past orders. However, the members of the Committee were courteous; they had not yet heard all the grumbling and suspicions and insinuations of disgruntled soldiers.

While the Joint Committee was interrogating witnesses about the battle, Stone continued to do his duty. In spite of his concern about those who blamed him for Ball's Bluff, his quarrels with Governor Andrew and Senator Sumner, and his appearance before the Joint Committee, he still found time to think about the enemy. It must have been difficult.

On December 14 he had ascended in a balloon tethered at Edwards Ferry to observe what he could of the Confederate dispositions around Leesburg. The balloonist was Professor Thaddeus Sobieski Coulincourt Lowe, who called himself "Chief Aeronaut, U.S. Army." Stone was the first general officer in this war (and perhaps any previous war) to go aloft in an observation balloon. His aerial observations, and what he learned from spies, scouts, deserters, and from newspapers and letters that passed over the river, enabled him to put before McClellan in January a plan for another attack across the Potomac. The Confederate forces opposite him, now commanded by Brigadier General D.H. Hill, were at the same time planning an attack on Stone. Neither attack was carried out. Stone was never told why his plan was rejected. On January 27, 1862, he was simply informed that it could not be "carried into effect at present" and he was ordered "to make no movement across the river until further orders." By this date a noose was tightening around the neck of the unsuspecting Stone.

It was on the evening of that same day that Senator Chandler and Congressmen Gooch and Julian called on the recently appointed Secretary of War to tell him of their suspicions concerning Stone. It was not the first time Stanton had met with members of the Committee. Ben Wade was an old friend for whom Stanton had done favors in the past. On the very day he took office as Secretary of War he had met with the entire Joint Committee on the Conduct of the War and told them: "We must strike hands and, uniting our strength and thought, double the power of government to suppress its enemies and restore its integrity." Later Stanton was secretly to pass on to Wade and other Republican senators information from War Department files which aided them in a campaign to smear West Pointers.

On January 28 Stanton informed McClellan of the "evidence" against Stone and handed him a handwritten order for Stone's arrest. McClellan protested that Stone should be given an opportunity to answer the charges against him. Reluctantly, Stanton agreed to approach Wade and request a second hearing. On January 31 Stone again appeared in the Committee's room in the Capitol's basement.

Stone was not told the names of his accusers. He was not even told what, specifically, he was accused of having done or not done. Senator Wade informed him in a general way of the accusations which had been made:

> *In the course of our investigation there has come out in evidence matters which may be said to impeach you. I do not know that I can enumerate all the points, but I think I can. In the first place is your conduct in the Ball's Bluff affair—your ordering your forces over without sufficient means of transportation, and in that way, of course, endangering your army, in case of check, by not being able to reinforce them. . . . We deem that the testimony tends also to impeach you for not reinforcing those troops when they were over there, in the face of the enemy. . . . Another point is, you are apparently impeached, I say "impeached." The evidence tends to prove that you have had undue communication with the enemy by letters that have passed back and forth, by intercourse with officers of the other side, and by permitting packages to go over unexamined to known Secessionists. . . . The next and only other point that now occurs to me is, that you have suffered the enemy to erect fortifications or batteries on the opposite side of the river, within reach of your guns, and that you could easily have prevented.*

From the tone of Stone's replies to the Committee's questions, it is obvious that he had no inkling that he was in imminent danger of arrest and imprisonment. Even had he known, he would have felt certain that no court could convict him, for he was innocent of any crime. All the charges made against him were only in general terms, his replies were, necessarily, also in general terms. His attitude was one of hurt indignation. He was incensed that his loyalty was questioned: "That is one humiliation I had hoped I should never be subjected to. . . . I thought there was one calumny that could not be brought against me." Stone reminded the Committee that he had raised the volunteer force for the defense of Washington and declared, quite rightly: "I could have surrendered Washington."

The tone of the Committee was definitely hostile and Stone was bitter. He invited the Committee to visit Edwards Ferry and see the situation there for themselves. Wade replied: "We are not military men, any of us."

"But you judge military men," said Stone.

"Yes sir," Wade responded, "but not finally. We only state what, in our opinion, tends to impeach them, when the evidence seems to do so, and then leave it to better judges to determine."

Stone did his best to explain the realities of his situation. As for the charge of undue communication with the enemy, he pointed out that McClellan had given permission for him to communicate with the Confederates under flags of truce, that he had accepted letters from Confederates to their prisoners in the North and had sent over letters addressed to Union prisoners of war. All letters received were sent to Washington. He had also, he said, permitted "a few, a very few" letters from civilians to be sent across the river after he had read them. Letters that were treasonable he burned. Through his communications with the enemy he had obtained valuable information he maintained, and he gave examples. "I have, so help me Heaven, but one object in all this," he said, "and that is to see the United States successful. . . . I have been as faithful as I can be. And I am exceedingly sore at this outrageous charge."

As to permitting the enemy to construct earthworks, Stone explained the futility of bombarding unmanned earthworks and declared that he was not going to waste shells costing the government five dollars each "simply to amuse the soldiers with the roar of artillery."

Wade answered, "When the evidence comes point blank from military men that the enemy are erecting formidable works that might have been prevented . . . of course we are bound to notice it."

Stone asked if the Committee's informants were artillery officers. Wade knew they were not, but he replied: "I do not know about that." Stone guessed they were not, but that probably they had, "like most volunteer infantry officers of little experience, supposed a gun would reach anywhere."

After hearing Stone's testimony, the Committee decided to meet again with Stanton, and at eight o'clock on the evening of February 4 the full Committee, except for Johnson and Covode (who was sick), called on him. Exactly what was said or what portions of the testimony the Committee presented is unknown, but the meeting was "of some hours' duration" and clearly it was the adverse testimony that was emphasized.

On Wednesday, February 5, Stone was invited by the president to a reception at the White House. Senator James A. McDougall of California saw him there: "He was . . . mingling with his friends, receiving as much attention and as much consideration from all about him as any man present. All smiled upon him; that at least appeared before his face." Two evenings later, on Friday, February 7, he was the guest of General McClellan. The following day he was at the War Department and spoke with Stanton. He asked if it would not be a good idea to have an official inquiry made into his conduct. Stanton told him: "There is no occasion for your inquiry; go back to your command." But Stone never returned to his command. Shortly after midnight on that very night he was arrested.

Exactly what discussions took place at the War Department in the week following Stone's second appearance before the Joint Committee and his arrest are unknown. McClellan still held Stanton's order for Stone's arrest, but he had told Stanton that there was insufficient evidence to frame charges. Then, on Saturday, February 8, McClellan received a written report of the interrogation of a refugee from Leesburg. Thirteen months later, McClellan told the Joint Committee about it:

> *There were in it statements which the refugee said he had heard made by the rebel officers, showing that a great deal of personal intercourse existed between them and General Stone. I think it was also stated that General Evans, then the rebel commander there, had received letters from General Stone; and there was a general expression on the part of those rebel officers of great cordiality towards Stone—confidence in him.*

Although he did not consider the charges substantial, McClellan, who said he knew only "in general terms what was the nature of the evidence taken by the Committee," thought the statement important enough to show to Stanton, who acted immediately. He ordered Stone's arrest.

McClellan wrote two orders: the first was directed to Brigadier General Andrew Porter, the Provost Marshal, ordering that Stone be placed under arrest, retained in "close custody" and sent under guard to Fort Lafayette (a prison in the New York Harbor to which political prisoners were sent); the second was directed to the officer in charge of the prison, ordering him to "please confine General Stone in Fort Lafayette, allowing him the comforts due his rank, and allowing him no communication with any one by letter or otherwise, except under the usual supervision."

So it was that Brigadier General George Sykes, commander of the regular army infantry brigade in Washington, appeared with a squad of armed soldiers in the middle of the night at Stone's door. It had taken time for the orders to be passed from hand to hand and General Sykes's nickname was "Tardy

213

George." The bayonets at his back were the only visible authority he possessed to arrest the astonished Stone. His orders had been given to him verbally. When Stone asked the cause of his arrest, Sykes replied that he was perfectly ignorant of it. Stone and Sykes knew each other. They had been at West Point together (Stone in the class of 1845 and Sykes that of 1842), both had won brevets in the Mexican War, both had been promoted into the 14th U.S. Infantry, and both had been appointed brigadier general of volunteers the previous year. Sykes said later that the arrest of Stone was the most painful duty he had ever been called upon to perform.

On February 9 Stone was taken under guard to Fort Lafayette. His money was taken from him, his mail censured; no visitors were permitted. He was confined in a barracks room designed as quarters for enlisted men with a sentinel posted at the door. This was his home for the next forty-nine days.

14.
The American Dreyfus

✳✳✳

In 1862 the 79th Article of War stated that soldiers could be held without charges for only eight days unless for some good reason a court-martial could not be convened. Although there was no reason that a court could not have been easily assembled in Washington, Stone was confined in prisons for 189 days without any charges being preferred against him and without ever being told of what crimes he was accused.

At first the public reaction to his arrest was one of approval. As Congressman James G. Blaine later wrote: "General Stone was selected for the sacrifice and popular wrath was turned upon him with burning intensity." A soldier in the 15th Massachusetts wrote home: "The arrest of General Stone created considerable excitement in the camp, though the general expression is, 'served him right'." Most northern newspapers approved. The New York *Daily Tribune* said: "The Union-restoring, slavery-respecting, secession-excusing class denounce the arrest as an outrage and a mistake. The earnest friends of the war and upholders of Secretary Stanton's new policy of action hold it as the date of an era of responsibility that may save us from commanders' mistakes and waste of blood."

There was no formal announcement from the War Department, but someone there obviously leaked the never-stated charges against Stone, for newspapers throughout the

215

North printed substantially the same story, giving the same reasons for his arrest. Typical was the article in the *Hampshire Gazette and Northampton Courier* of Northampton, Massachusetts, on February 11:

> *The following is the substance of the charges against him: First, misbehavior at the Battle of Ball's Bluff; second, holding correspondence with the enemy before and since the Battle of Ball's Bluff, and receiving rebel officers in his camp; third, treacherously suffering the enemy to build a fort and erecting works since the Battle of Ball's Bluff, under his guns without molestation; fourth, for a treacherous design of leading his force to capture and destruction by the enemy under pretense of orders for a movement from the commanding general, which had not been given. A court-martial will be speedily ordered.*

The morning after his arrest, Stone sent a note to General Seth Williams, McClellan's adjutant general, whom he knew from West Point and service in the Mexican War; Stone informed him of his arrest and added: "Conscious of having been at all times a faithful soldier of the United States, I most respectfully request that I may be furnished at as early a moment as practicable with a copy of whatever charges may have been preferred against me, with the opportunity of promptly meeting them." He was given no answer.

When his frequent requests to the War Department for a statement of the charges against him were ignored and when his demands for a trial were brushed aside, Stone appears to have realized that the source of his troubles was political and that his only hope for justice lay in help from political friends. Fortunately, he was not without such friends.

On February 16 Joseph Bradley, a future associate justice of the Supreme Court, wrote to Stanton, saying: "General Stone I rank among my friends. I believe in his integrity and fidelity. So fully do I believe that scarcely anything could shake the belief. He has served me as a friend and I want to let him know how truly I sympathize with him. I enclose an open letter for him which I desire you to read, and unless there is something objectionable in it which I cannot see do me the favor to have it forwarded to him."

Bradley's letter to Stone confirmed his belief in Stone's innocence. Offering his help, he wrote that he was sure Stone would not be denied a fair trail, for "there are too many persons feeling a deep and lively interest in your fate, you have since this rebellion broke out made too many friends, and the public interest is too deeply involved in the issues connected with your arrest and imprisonment." Four days later Bradley was informed that Stanton thought the letter was "an improper one to be sent to General Stone" and that he was therefore withholding it. Bradley had also requested permission to visit Stone. It was refused.

Henry M. Parker, a Massachusetts lawyer who undertook to represent Stone, tried in vain to see Stanton. For more than a week Stanton refused to talk to him; finally he made an appointment, and then broke it. Not until February 19 did Stanton speak briefly with him and then he gave little satisfaction. He insisted that there was nothing "extraordinary" about Stone's case which would entitle it to precedence in his attention or to induce him rapidly to conclude it. Stanton's attitude, as he later expressed it, was that "individuals are nothing; we are contributing thousands of them to save the Union, and General Stone in Fort Lafayette is doing his share in that direction."

The day after this unsatisfactory interview, Parker wrote to Stanton requesting the return of Stone's papers and personal possessions and complaining that "neither General Stone nor his family nor his counsel can be allowed to know either his accusers or what the accusations against him are." Stanton ignored him.

Parker originally suspected that Senator Sumner was re-

sponsible for Stone's arrest. In view of the bitter feud between
the two men, it was a natural assumption. Sumner certainly
had no love for Stone, but he vigorously denied newspaper
reports that he had arranged for his arrest; he declared that
the step was taken without his "suggestion or hint, direct or
indirect." Indeed, Sumner was innocent and, in fact, stated
his own belief that Stone ought to be confronted by his accusers and given a trial at an early date.

On March 15 a doctor reported that Stone was being kept
in too close confinement and that his health was suffering.
On March 28 Stanton ordered him to be transferred to Fort
Hamilton on the mainland and to be allowed some exercise.
Two days later Stone asked if his wife, Maria, could join him;
a week later he was told that his request was denied. He then
applied to serve "in any capacity whatever" with the Union
forces before Yorktown. He received no response.

Meanwhile, powerful friends in the Congress set to work
on his behalf. On March 24 Senator Milton S. Latham, Senator James A. McDougall and Congressman Aaron A. Sargent
sent a strong memorial to Secretary Stanton asserting that
"the long arrest of General Stone without military trial or
inquiry has led to complaints from many quarters." They added
that "having known General Stone for years, and never having
had cause to doubt his loyalty, we feel it our duty to inquire
of the government through you for some explanation of a
proceeding which seems to us most extraordinary."

Stanton did not bother to reply. Three times Senator
McDougall personally went to the War Department and tried
to see Stanton. Each time he was turned away. Alarmed by
the audacity of the man, he told the Senate: "Strange times
have come upon the land when the Secretaries of the president
deny the right of Senators to official intercourse." After three
frustrating weeks he introduced into the Senate a resolution
of inquiry: The Secretary of War was requested to say upon
whose complaint Stone had been arrested; to explain why he

had been denied his rights under the Articles of War; why no charges had been filed; why Stone had not been informed of the charges; to ask whether any charges were being prepared; and under what pretense he was still confined in prison. The resolution was debated in the Senate on April 15, 16 and 22.

McDougall, a Democrat from California, not only demanded that justice be done to Stone but that Secretary of War Stanton be brought to heel. Stone, he said, "has been wronged and outraged by a government official." He accused Stanton himself of violating the Articles of War and of undertaking to make law, "the tyrant's law—the law of power, which one man may possess and exercise without limitation and without authority." Stanton, he stormed, was "restrained by no rule fixed in any statute book" and was attempting to conceal his crimes because of "fear, coward fear."

He lashed out at Wade as well. Wade had called McDougall a traitor for defending Stone and had said that "the man who invokes the Constitution in forbearance of the law to punish traitors is himself a sympathizer." This was fairly standard Wade logic. Speaking to the Senate, McDougall compared Wade to Torquemada and his committee to the Inquisition. "In this country, which is called free, these are strange things," he said, "strange things to be done in the name of constitutional liberty."

In the end, McDougall's resolution was considerably watered down and reduced to a mere request to the president of the United States that he "communicate to the Senate any information touching the imprisonment of General Stone not deemed incompatible with the public interest." This was adopted on April 21, 1862.

On May 1 Lincoln made his reply. The president's role in the Stone affair, if not culpable, was certainly not creditable. In extenuation, it must be said that at the time of Stone's arrest two of Lincoln's children were sick, and on February 20 Willie Lincoln died. Later Lincoln wrote: "Owing to sickness in my family, the Secretary of War made the arrest without notifying me that he had it in contemplation." When Stanton did tell him of Stone's arrest, Lincoln said: "I suppose you have good reason for it; and having good reason, I am glad I knew nothing of it until it was done." Lincoln was to retain this head-in-the-sand attitude throughout the affair.

It is possible that although Lincoln might have considered Stone to be loyal, he still believed him to be responsible for the death of his friend. Edward B. Jerome, son of Baker's sister, Rebecca, told a story twenty years later of how he and his uncle, Dr. Alfred Baker, had called on the president and had shown him the blood-stained order from Stone that had been found in Baker's hat after his death. According to Jerome, Lincoln said, "Gentlemen, my Baker was murdered." Although this story is suspect, it might well reflect Lincoln's feelings at the time.

As his reply to the Senate's request for information, Lincoln sent a letter that would appear to have been drafted for him by the War Department:

> In relation to Brigadier General Stone, I have the honor to state that he was arrested and imprisoned under my general authority, and upon evidence which, whether he be guilty or innocent, required, as appeared to me, such proceedings to be had against him for the public safety. I deem it incompatible with the public interest, as also, perhaps, unjust to General Stone, to make a more particular statement of the evidence.

> He has not been tried because, in the state of military operations at the time of his arrest and since, the officers to constitute a court-martial and for witnesses could not be withdrawn from duty without serious injury to the service. He will be allowed a trial without any unnecessary delay; the charges

*and specifications will be furnished him in due sea-
son, and every facility for his defense will be offered
him by the War Department.*

Lincoln may have believed the War Department's protes-
tation, but there was no excuse whatever for not bringing
Stone speedily to trial; no charges or specification were ever
shown to him; he was not brought to trial "without unnecessary delay," and certainly not given "every facility for his
defense." On July 4, 1862, Stone wrote directly to president
Lincoln. He received no reply.

An act of the Congress, passed on July 17, finally procured
Stone's release. To a bill "defining the pay and emoluments
of certain officers," a proviso was added making it unlawful
to hold an officer under arrest for more than thirty days without bringing him to trial. Even then the War Department
dragged its feet, choosing to interpret the act as giving it the
right to keep Stone imprisoned for thirty days after the passage
of the law. Consequently, he was not set free until August
16.

Stone, never having been tried or convicted of any crime,
being still a colonel in the regular army and a brigadier general
of volunteers, immediately reported for duty. No assignment
was given him; the adjutant general informed him that no
orders had been issued concerning him. Stone then applied
to General McClellan, then about to fight the bloodiest battle
of the war at Antietam. McClellan wrote on September 7 to
Secretary Stanton, saying that he would like to make use of
Stone's services and adding that he had "no doubt as to his
loyalty and devotion." But not even McClellan could elicit
a reply from Stanton.

On September 25 Stone wrote to then General-in-Chief
Halleck and again asked for a copy of the charges against him
and for an opportunity to answer those charges and to confront
his accusers. He reminded Halleck that it had been 228 days

since his arrest, and he asked for a trial before all of the witnesses were dead or scattered. General Halleck replied that he knew of no charges and that he had no official information as to why he was arrested.

On December 1, 1862, Stone, still without employment, again wrote to McClellan, calling his attention to the Act of July 17 and noting that as McClellan had been the arresting officer he was obliged to furnish a copy of the charges. In reply, McClellan told Stone of Stanton's handwritten order for his arrest and of Stanton's statement that it had been issued at the solicitation of the Joint Committee on the Conduct of the War. He also told Stone of the statement by the Leesburg refugee.

This was the first time Stone had heard of the Leesburg refugee who triggered his arrest. When he asked for a copy of his statement and his name, McClellan answered that he had forgotten the name; his report, he said, had been sent to the War Department. On April 13 Stone requested the War Department furnish him a copy of the report, but Stanton refused to give it to him. The report has never been found. To this day, nothing is known of the Leesburg refugee.

Two years after the Battle of Ball's Bluff the mood of the country changed. There was a general feeling that Stone had been wronged; no one now wanted to claim responsibility for his arrest. Wade and his colleagues were now anxious to counter charges that they had been Stone's nemesis, and Wade wrote that Stanton had been told only that "the testimony upon the points to which his attention had been called was conflicting." Wade was to claim in the Committee's first report that they had "made no recommendation as to what should be done, one way or the other; merely reporting to him that the testimony was conflicting." According to Wade, the Committee had been surprised at the extent of their own influence.

Stone wrote again to the president, asking if he could "inform me why I was sent to Fort Lafayette." Lincoln replied that he could not tell him much and referred him to General Henry Wager Halleck. But Halleck said the arrest was made on the recommendation of McClellan. McClellan pointed the finger at Stanton, who now in aggrieved tones said that McClellan himself had recommended the arrest and "now seemed to be pushing the whole thing on my shoulders."

On January 8, 1863, Stone asked for the return of his personal papers and possessions that had been confiscated at the time of his arrest. Brigadier General Gorman had reported to Washington on February 10, 1862—two days after Stone's arrest—that he had placed all of Stone's private and official papers, together with his personal possessions, under strict guard, both "from a sense of duty to the public service and his own defense." He added that all would be sealed in the presence of General Banks, Colonel Devens and Colonel Dana; he would then, he said, "await further orders." It would appear that they were sent to Washington and then disappeared. Although two weeks after making his request for the return of his papers and property he was told that they would be returned to him, they never were.

On February 27, 1863, nearly five months after his release from prison, Stone made his third and last appearance before the Joint Committee on the Conduct of the War. For the first time he was allowed to read the transcript of the testimony and to learn who had spoken against him and what they had said. He was then able to answer each accusation in detail with convincing candor and clarity.

The Joint Committee was now eager to demonstrate that it had played little or no part in his arrest and that if its members had once entertained suspicions of Stone's loyalty they had had good reasons. When Stone finished responding to the accusatory testimony, Ben Wade asked innocently: "Why did you not give us these explanations when you were here before?"

Stone, with commendable restraint, reminded Wade and

his committee that "the Committee did not state to me the particular cases." He had, he said, merely given "general answers to general questions." He also explained to the Committee why he had not demanded a court of inquiry: "While General McClellan was at Edwards Ferry, he showed me a telegram he had written to the president to the effect that he had examined into the affair at Ball's Bluff and that General Stone was entirely without blame." He explained that in view of this it would not have been respectful for him to ask for a court of inquiry: "It was given by the highest authority and sent to the highest authority, and as a soldier I had no right to ask for justification except from my superiors."

Stone's persecution did not end with his release from prison: even when he was eventually given employment, he was never promoted and he was never given another command. On May 3, 1863, he was at last restored to duty and sent to the Department of the Gulf to serve on the staff of Major General Nathaniel Banks, a former governor of Massachusetts. In this capacity he served in the Port Hudson and the disastrous Red River campaigns, taking part in the fighting at Bayou Teche, Sabine Cross Roads and Pleasant Hill. Banks was sympathetic to Stone's plight and he personally wrote to Lincoln, enclosing a letter from Stone to the president in which he begged that "some act, some word, some order, may issue from the executive which shall place my name clear of reproach."

There exists an unfinished draft of a letter Lincoln began in response to Bank's request. Its general tenor was that Lincoln knew of no conclusive evidence against Stone but that he agreed with Stanton that "to hold one commander in prison untried is less harmful in times of great national distress than to withdraw several good officers from active battle-fields to give him a trial." Lincoln must have realized what an unconvincing argument this was; there were a great many general officers, particularly in Washington, who were not actively engaged on the battlefield.

Congressman James G. Blaine, writing of the Stone affair twenty years later, noted:

> *No reparation to him for the protracted defamation of his character, no order was published acknowledging that he was found guiltless, no communication was ever made to him by National authority giving even a hint of the grounds on which for half a year he was pilloried before the nation as a malefactor. The wound which General Stone received was deep.*

General Banks was well pleased to have Stone on his staff, but mysteriously, Stone was recalled on orders from Washington. No explanation was given. Although briefly assigned to the Army of the Potomac, he was sick and in despair over the malignant forces working against him. On April 14, 1864, he resigned as a brigadier general of volunteers, and on September 13 he resigned his regular army commission as colonel of the 14th United States Infantry.

When the war was over, he found employment as engineer and superintendent of the Dover Coal Mines Company near what is today the village of Manakin in Goochland County, Virginia. He remained here from 1865 until 1869, and it was apparently during this period that his first wife, Maria Louisa, died. In 1867 he married Annie Jeanie Stone, daughter of John H. Stone of Louisiana, by whom he had a son, John, born on September 24, 1869.

Stone's luck appeared to have changed. The mining operations were successful and he prospered. For the blacks in the community he built a large brick church, and for himself he built a house some envious neighbors considered "pretentious," but when the Chesapeake and Ohio Railroad was built, it flooded the mine's marketing area with cheaply-mined coal from the Appalachian Mountains. The Dover Coal Mine

Company failed and Stone fell into debt. On March 30, 1870, Stone signed a five-year contract with the Khedive of Egypt to serve as an officer in the Egyptian army. Some fifty former officers, both Union and Confederate, signed similar contracts. Of these, fifteen were West Point graduates, seven were Annapolis graduates, and one was a graduate of the Virginia Military Institute. Among these American officers in the Egyptian army, most of whom served under Stone, was Walter Jenifer, the Confederate cavalry officer who was one of the senior battlefield commanders who helped defeat Baker's force at Ball's Bluff.

By 1879 all of the Americans except Stone had left the Khedival service. Stone, still in debt, stayed on; by this time he was a pasha and chief of staff of the Egyptian army, a position he retained until the British conquest of Egypt in 1882. Early in 1883 he returned to the United States. After working for a year as the chief engineer for the Florida Ship Canal Company, he was employed as the constructing engineer to build the great pedestal for the Statue of Liberty in the same New York harbor where he had been so unjustly imprisoned more than twenty years earlier.

Stone Pasha died in New York City on January 24, 1887, the result, it was said, of riding bareheaded in the rain during the parade that preceded the ceremonies marking the dedication of the monument by Grover Cleveland on October 28, 1886.

Congressman Blaine believed that "His case will stand as a warning against future violations of the liberty which is the birthright of every American and against the danger of appeasing popular clamor by the sacrifice of an innocent man."

After Lincoln's assassination, when Andrew Johnson, one of the original members of the Joint Committee, became the 17th president of the United States, his attempts to carry out Lincoln's reconstruction and reconciliation policies brought him into conflict with Ben Wade and other Radical Republicans who were eager to humiliate the South and make it suffer. On August 12, 1867, Johnson dismissed the egregious Edwin Stanton as Secretary of War and replaced him, ad interim, with General U.S. Grant. The Senate, however, declared this executive act illegal under the Tenure of Office Act of March 2, 1867, requiring the approval of the Senate for the replacement of a cabinet officer. Grant went back to being a soldier, and Stanton returned to the War Office.

On February 21, 1868, President Johnson again tried to rid himself of Stanton, and this time to replace him with Brevet Major General Lorenzo Thomas. Three days later impeachment proceedings against him were instituted in the House of Representatives, charging him with "high crimes and misdemeanors," and there was a long list of specifications, (called articles of impeachment). On March 13 the trial of the president of the United States by the Senate opened with Chief Justice Salmon Portland Chase presiding; it ended on May 26.

A two-thirds majority on any article of impeachment was necessary to convict. As the Constitution of the United States then stood, the Congress could by law provide a president when there was neither an eligible president nor vice president, and under a law passed on March 1, 1792, the next in line of succession after the president and vice president was the president of the Senate pro tempore. As there was no vice president, Ben Wade, then the president of the Senate pro tem., would become president if Johnson was convicted. It was rumored as the trial began that Wade had already begun to select his Cabinet. On two articles the vote was 35 guilty to 19 not guilty—only one vote short of the number needed to convict. Thus, Bluff Ben Wade became the only man in history ever to have failed to become president by a single vote.

Selected Bibliography

Anon. *The Association of the Graduates of the United States Military Academy Annual Reunion, June 9th, 1887.* Evening News Printing and Binding House, East Saginaw, Michigan, 1887.

Anon. *The Confederate Soldier in the Civil War.* Pageant Books, Patterson, New Jersey, 1959.

Anon. *Contributions to the History of the Richmond Howitzer Battalion.* "Extracts from an 'Old Order Book' of the First Company, Richmond Howitzers." Pamphlets 4&5, J.W. Randolf & English, Richmond, Virginia, 1886.

Anon. *History of the Nineteenth Regiment Massachusetts Volunteer Infantry.* (Issued by the History Committee.) Salem Press, Salem, Massachusetts, 1906.

Anon. *Loudoun County and the Civil War.* Civil War Centenial Commission, 1965.

Anon. *A Memorial of Paul Joseph Revere and Edward H.R. Revere.* Privately printed. Wm. Parsons Lunt, Boston, 1874.

Baltz, John D. *Hon. Edward D. Baker.* Published for the author by Inquirer Printing Co., Lancaster, Pennsylvania, 1888.

Banes, Charles H. *History of the Philadelphia Brigade.* Lippincott, Philadelphia, Pennsylvania, 1876.

Basler, Ray P. (ed.) *The Collected Works of Abraham Lincoln.* 8 vols. Rutgers University Press, New Brunswick, New Jersey, 1953.

Blackford, Charles M. (ed.) *Letters from Lee's Army.* Scribner's Sons, New York, 1947.

Blaine, James G. *Twenty Years of Congress: From Lincoln to Garfield.* 2 vols. Henry Bill, Norwich, Connecticut, 1884.

Blair, Harry C. and Tarshis, Rebecca. *Lincoln's Constant Ally: The Life of Colonel Edward C. Baker.* Civil War Memorial publication by the Oregon Historical Society, Portland, Oregon, 1960.

Boatner, Mark Mayo. *The Civil War Dictionary.* David McKay, New York, 1959.

Bowen, Catherine Drinkwater. *Yankee from Olympus: Justice Holmes and His Family.* Little, Brown, Boston, 1945.

Bruce, George A. *The 20th Regiment of Massachusetts Volunteer Infantry.* Houghton Mifflin, Boston, 1906.

Catton, Bruce. *The Army of the Potomac: Glory Road.* Doubleday, Garden City, New York, 1952.

———— Mr. Lincoln's Army. Doubleday, Garden City, New York, 1951.

Commager, Henry Steele. *The Blue and the Gray.* V. 1. Bobbs-Merrill, Indianapolis & New York, 1950.

Copeland, R. Morris. "Statement of R. Morris Copeland." Pamphlet. Prenties & Deland, Boston, 1864.

Crabitès, Pierre. *Americans in the Egyptian Army.* George Routledge & Sons, London, 1938.

Crothy, Daniel G. *Four Years Campaigning in the Army of the Potomac.* Grand Rapids, Michigan, 1874.

Cuthbert, Norma B. *Lincoln and the Baltimore Plot.* Huntington Library, San Marino, California, 1949.

Davis, Burke. *Our Incredible Civil War.* Holt, Rinehart & Winston, New York, 1960.

Diehl, George West. *The True Confederate Soldier: Col. Elijah Viers.* Unpublished manuscript in Thomas Balch Library, Leesburg, Virginia.

Earle, Captain David M. *History of the Excursion of the Fifteenth Massachusetts Regiment. . .to the Battlefields of Gettysburg, Pa., Antietam, Md., Ball's Bluff, Virginia and Washington, D.C., May 31–June 12, 1886.* Charles Hamilton, Worcester, 1886.

Eliot, Ellsworth. *West Point in the Confederacy.* Baker, New York, 1941.

Fatout, Paul. "The California Regiment, Colonel Baker, and Ball's Bluff", *California Historical Society Quarterly*, Vol. xxxi, No. 3, San Francisco, September 1952.

Foner, Jack D. *Blacks and the Military in American History.* Praeger, New York and Washington, 1974.

Foote, Shelby. *The Civil War: A Narrative.* 4 vols. Random House, New York, 1958.

Ford, Andrew E. *The Story of the 15th Regiment Massachusetts Volunteer Infantry in the Civil War.* Clinton, Massachusetts, 1898.

Haskell, John. *The Haskell Memoirs.* (Edited by Gilbert E. Govon and James W. Livingood.) G.P. Putnam's Sons, New York, 1960.

Head, James W. *History and Comprehensive Description of Loudoun County Virginia.* Park View Press, n.p., 1908.

Heilman, Francis B. *Historical Register and Dictionary of the United States Army.* 2 vols. Government Printing Office, Washington, D.C., 1903.

Hensford, Mrs. P.A. *The Young Captain: A Memorial of Capt. Richard C. Derby.* Degen, Estes & Co., Boston, 1865.

Hill, Richard. *Biographical Dictionary of the Anglo-Egyptian Sudan.* Oxford University Press, Oxford, 1951.

Holcombe, R.I. *History of the First Regiment Minnesota Volunteer Infantry.* Easton and Masterman, Stillwater, Minnesota, 1916.

Howe, Mark De Wolfe. *Justice Holmes: the Shaping Years.* Harvard University Press, Cambridge, Massachusetts, 1957.

—— *Touched With Fire: Civil War Letters and Diary of Oliver Wendell Holmes, 1861–1864.* Harvard University Press, Cambridge, Massachusetts, 1946.

Hunton, Eppa. *The Autobiography of Eppa Hunton.* The William Byrd Press, Richmond, Virginia, 1933.

Irwin, Richard B. *Battles and Leaders of the Civil War.* 4 vols. Thomas Yoseloff, New York, 1956. (Originally printed in 1884–87.)

Jones, Katherine M. *Heroines of Dixie.* Bobbs-Merrill, Indianapolis and New York, 1955.

Jones, Virgil Carrington. *The Civil War at Sea.* Holt, Rinehart & Winston, New York, 1960.

—— *Gray Ghosts and Rebel Raiders.* Henry Holt, New York, 1956.

Kane, Harnett T. *Spies for the Blue and Gray.* Hanover House, Garden City, New York, 1954.

Kennedy, Elijah R. *The Contest for California in 1861: How Colonel E.D. Baker Saved the Pacific States to the Union.* Houghton Mifflin, Boston and New York, 1912.

Lee, Thomas Amory. "Brevet-Brigadier General William Raymond Lee." (Pamphlet reprint from *Colonial Families of the United States of America*, Vol. 5) n.p., n.d.

Leech, Margaret. *Reveille in Washington, 1860–1865.* Harper & Row, New York, 1941.

Lenman, Charles (ed.) *Journal of Alfred Ely, a Prisoner of War in Richmond.* D. Appleton, New York, 1862.

Levine, Benjamin, and Story, Isabelle F. "Statue of Liberty National Monument." Pamphlet. *National Park Service Historical Handbook*, Series No. 11, Washington, D.C., 1961.

Lowell, Colonel Charles Russell. *Memoirs of the War of '61.* George H. Ellis, Boston, 1920.

McClellan, George B. *McClellan's Own Story.* Charles L. Webster, New York, 1887.

McDougall, J.A. "Speech of Hon. J.A. McDougall on the Arrest of Gen. Stone and the Rights of the Soldier and the Citizen." Delivered in the Senate of the United States, April 15, 16 & 22, 1862. Pamphlet, L. Tower & Co., Washington, D.C., 1862.

Macon, T.J. *Reminiscences of the First Company of Richmond Howitzers.* Whittet & Shepperson, Richmond, Virginia, n.d.

Marvin, Abijah. *History of Worcester in the War of the Rebellion.* Published by the author, Worcester, 1880.

Mitchell, Lieutenant Colonel Joseph B. "Debacle at Ball's Bluff." *Civil War Times Illustrated,* January 1962.

Morison, Samuel Eliot, and Commager, Henry Steele. *The Growth of the American Republic.* 2 vols. Oxford University Press, New York, 1942.

Myres, Frank M. *The Comanches: A History of White's Battalion, Virginia Cavalry.* Kelly, Piet & Co., Baltimore, 1871.

Nevins, Allen. *The War for the Union.* v.1. Charles Scribner's Sons, New York, 1959.

Nicolay, John G. and Hay, J. (eds.) *Complete Works of Abraham Lincoln.* 12 vols. Lincoln Memorial University, 1894.

Palfrey, Francis Winthrop. "In Memoriam, H.L.A." [Henry L. Abbott] Pamphlet printed for private distribution. Boston, 1864.

———— *Memoir for William Francis Bartlett.* Houghton, Osgood & Co., Boston, 1878.

Patch, Joseph D. *The Battle of Ball's Bluff.* Potomac Press, Leesburg, Virginia, 1958.

Peirson, Charles Lawrence. *Ball's Bluff.* Privately printed. Salem Press, Salem, Massachusetts, 1913.

Pierson, W.W. "The Committee on the Conduct of the War." *American Historical Review,* vol. xxiii.

Pollard, E.A. *Southern History of the War: The First Year of the War.* West & Johnston, Richmond, Virginia, 1862. Reprinted and corrected: Charles B. Richardson, New York, 1864.

Pratt, Fletcher. *Stanton: Lincoln's Secretary of War.* W.W. Norton, New York, 1953.

Prince, Ezra M. "The Fourth Illinois Infantry in the War with Mexico." *Illinois Historical Society Transactions,* 1906.

Ramey, Emily, and Gott, John K. (eds.) *The Years of Anguish: Fauquier County, Virginia, 1861–1865.* Printed in the shop of the *Fauquier Democrat,* Warren, Virginia, 1959, for the Fauquier County Civil War Centennial Committee.

Randall, J.G. and Donald, David. *The Civil War and Reconstruction.* Little Brown, Boston, 1869.

Reid, Whitelaw. *Ohio in the War: Her Statesmen and Her Generals and Her Soldiers.* 2 vols. Moore, Wilstach and Baldwin, New York, 1868.

Revere, Joseph W. *Keel and Saddle.* Osgood, Boston, 1872.

Sandburg, Carl. *Abraham Lincoln: The War Years.* 2 vols. Harcourt, Brace & Co., New York, 1939.

Sargent, Horace Binney. "Memorial Address Delivered before the John Albion Monument Association, Hingham, October 8, 1863." Pamphlet. Rockwell and Churchill, Boston, 1875.

Schouler, William. *A History of Massachusetts in the Civil War.* 2 vols. E.P. Dutton, Boston, 1868.

Silver, James W. (ed.) *A Life for the Confederacy as Recorded in the Pocket Diaries of Pvt. Robert A. Moore.* McCowat-Mercer, Jackson, Tennessee, 1959.

Smith, Jean H. *Snickersville.* Booklet. Printed by *Miamisburg News,* Miamisburg, Ohio. n.d.

Stern, Philip Van Dorn. *The Confederate Navy: A Pictorial History.* Doubleday, New York, 1962.

Stiles, Robert. *Four Years Under Marse Robert.* Neals Publishing Co., New York & Washington, 1903.

Stone, Charles P. "Washington in 1861." *Magazine of American History,* July 1884.

Taylor, Frank H. *Philadelphia in the Civil War, 1861–1865.* Published by the City, Philadelphia, 1913.

Thomas, Benjamin P. and Hynan, Harold M. *Stanton: The Life and Times of Lincoln's Secretary of War.* Knopf, New York, 1962.

Thomas, Clarence. *General Turner Ashby.* Privately published. Winchester, Virginia, 1907.

Westwood, Howard C. "The Joint Committee on the Conduct of the War—A Look at the Record." *Lincoln Herald,* Spring, 1978. Vol. 80, No. 1.

White, E.V. "History of the Battle of Ball's Bluff." Bulletin of the Loudoun County Historical Society, Vol. iv, 1965. Leesburg, Virginia.

Wiley, Bell Irvin. *The Common Soldier in the Civil War.* Grosset & Dunlop, New York, 1951.

Willis, Henry A. *Fitchburg in the War of the Rebellion.* Stephen Shipley, Fitchburg, Massachusetts, 1866.

Williams, T. Harry. "Investigation: 1862." *American Heritage,* December 1954.

Wilson, Mrs. H. Neill. "Sketch of the Life of Gen. William F. Bartlett." Collection of the Berkshire Historical Society, Vol. 2, No. 4, 1913.

Wistar, Isaac Jones. *Autobiography of Isaac Jones Wistar, 1827–1905.* The Wistar Institute of Anatomy and Biology, Philadelphia, 1937.

Woodward, William E. *Years of Madness.* G.P. Putnam's Sons, New York, 1951.

Worthington, C.J. (ed.) *The Woman in Battle: A Narrative of the Exploits, Adventures and Travels of Madame Loreta Janeta Velazquez.* T. Belnap, Hartford, 1876.

Anonymous U.S. Government Publications:

Report of the Joint Committee on the Conduct of the War. 3 vols., G.P.O., Washington, D.C., 1863.

The War of the Rebellion: A Compilation of the Official Records of the Union and Confederate Armies. 128 vols. G.P.O. (The first four volumes are of particular interest.)

Index

OTHER EPM MILITARY BOOKS

GRAY GHOSTS AND REBEL RAIDERS
by Virgil Carrington Jones $14.95

This first quality-paperback edition of the 1956 bestseller tells the story of
the Confederate guerrillas who, without ever fighting a major battle, pro-
longed the Civil War many months through their daring, unpredictable attacks behind enemy lines. They rode off with supply wagons, horses and
guns, destroyed bridges and railroads, and intercepted secret messages. Author is a veteran journalist and well-known Civil War historian. 431 pages.

RANGER MOSBY
by Virgil Carrington Jones $14.95

A national bestseller when it first appeared in 1944 and in print ever since,
this is the definitive biography of the crafty, flamboyant Civil War irregular
whose midnight raids presaged guerrilla tactics of the 20th century. During
the years 1864–1865, Colonel John S. Mosby and his Rebel Rangers tor-
mented Union troops in northern Virginia by penetrating enemy camps,
kidnapping a general, and robbing a federal payroll train. Despite a bounty
for his head, Mosby escaped the 5,000 Union troops sent to capture him.
347 pages/photographs.

MILITARY LEADERS IN THE CIVIL WAR
by Joseph B. Mitchell $10.95

Against the backdrop of climactic events and decisions, West Point graduate
and historian Mitchell offers concise, provocative profiles of ten important
Civil War generals, including Grant, Lee and Sherman, and evaluates the
strategies each man employed and their individual talents and weaknesses.
These provocative essays tell us much about success and failure, not only in
war, but in any endeavor. 251 pages/photographs/maps.

MILITARY LEADERS IN THE AMERICAN
REVOLUTION
by Joseph B. Mitchell $10.95

In the vivid style that has made his books popular for three decades, Mitchell gives the true and dramatic story of ten generals in the American Revo-
lution, six American and four British, fighting a war with oddly mixed
armies of fluctuating size, loyalties and experience and tells us what they
thought and did and why. 223 pages/maps.

MR. LINCOLN'S CITY: An Illustrated Guide to the Civil War Sites of Washington
by Richard M. Lee $17.95

This pictorial history and guide to the nation's capital as it was between those tumultuous, tragic years 1861–1865 will lead you to hospitals and homes that still exist and such sites as Congressman Abe Lincoln's boarding house; fascinating wartime photographs and drawings recall vividly those that have passed from the scene. 176 pages/photographs/illustrations/maps.

GENERAL LEE'S CITY: An Illustrated Guide to the Historic Sites of Confederate Richmond
by Richard M. Lee $16.95

Confederate Richmond is recaptured in dramatic detail through scores of photographs, drawings, maps and first-hand accounts, Poignant stories of individual courage and heroism are mixed with descriptions of daily activities and turmoil in the fledgling Confederate government; a gripping tale of a city under siege. 184 pages/photographs/illustrations/maps.

A FEW GREAT CAPTAINS: The Men and Events That Shaped the Development of U.S. Air Power
by DeWitt S. Copp $19.95

A superb account of the evolution of U.S. air power is also the story of four bold men—H.H. "Hap" Arnold, Frank M. Andrews, Carl Spaatz and Ira C. Eaker—and many others who shared their dream of conquering the skies and whose dedication eventually produced the most powerful striking force in the world. 531 pages/photographs.

Order Blank for all EPM books described here. Mail with check to:

EPM Publications, Box 490, McLean, VA 22101

Title	Qty	Price	Amount

Subtotal _____

Virginia residents add $4\frac{1}{2}$% tax _____

Orders totaling up to $15 add $2 shipping/handling _____

Orders totaling more than $15 add $3 first item, $1 ea. add'l. _____

Total _____

Name _____

Street _____

City _____ State _____ Zip _____

Remember to enclose names, addresses and enclosure cards for gift purchases. Prices are subject to change. For free catalog call 1-800-289-2339.